THE PRO
O
ST. MAI
&
ST. COLUMBKILLE

by

PETER BANDER

and introductions

by

Archbishop H. E. Cardinale,
Canon W. Coslett Quin,
and Joel Wells

COLIN SMYTHE
GERRARDS CROSS

Printed in Great Britain
Printed and bound by The Guernsey Press Company Ltd.,
Vale, Guernsey, C.I.

PREFACE

by JOEL WELLS, Editor THE CRITIC

If this book does no more than give pause to those scoffers who customarily go about saying that the Prophecies of Malachy are nothing other than scurrilous rubbish, it will have accomplished a great deal—if only because there are so many people who tend to think this way. There is another group, of course, who have never heard of these famous foretellings of the popes by which the good Malachy undertook to list in advance the proper succession of Roman pontiffs from Celestine II (1143) to "the end of the world". He didn't just come right out and name them, of course. That would have taken all the sport out of it for one thing and, for another, would have considerably curtailed the free-will of the College of Cardinals. Quite sensibly, he chose to reveal the successors under symbolic titles, set down in Latin.

I belong to yet a third group—or belonged, I should say—who had heard of the Prophecies but had not bothered to think much about their validity one way or the other. I could, as so many of my contemporary indifferentists are wont to say, not have cared less. But count me among the utterly concerned and utterly converted. Peter Bander's commentary and interpretation of the prophecies have carried the day completely. So far as I'm concerned, there's not the least shadow of a doubt as to their authenticity.

The scoffers, of course, begin with the primary objection that these writings were not even "discovered" for some four-hundred odd years after Malachy's death in the year 1148. They object further that he would surely have told somebody about them, at least his dear friend St. Bernard of Clairvaux; they carp and twitter and nit-pick in other disagreeable and tendentious ways as well. But to no avail—the elegant and soaring scholarship of Peter Bander disposes of all these objections with authoritative dispatch. He remains too much the professional even to descend to the gut-level argument that I, laboring under no such restraining ethic, would have cited at once: namely, that Malachy was not only Irish, but an Irish saint, and the first Irishman to actually be canonized by formal process of the Church. Would such a man be apt to jeopardize his chances by leaving a notorious piece of scurrilous writing behind him?

There will be those, too, who say that it's easy enough to match up pope and prophetic clue after the fact. Thus we know that when Malachy wrote *Bos Albanus in Portu* that he was obviously referring to Rodrigo Borgia, Alexander VI (1492-1503), because of "the pope's armorial bearing and his Cardinal titles of Albano and Porto." He also behaved like a bull on more than a few occasions so that the prediction "the Alban bull at the port" is not only literally but allegorically accurate. But the wicked Alexander is grossly obvious; it takes a knowledge of the papacy amounting almost to an obsession—albeit a most lofty one—to realize that *Picus Inter Escas* (A woodpecker among the food) was going to turn out to be Nicholas IV.

Interest in the prophecies is somewhat cyclical in nature, tending to go up sharply when the reigning pontiff grows extremely old or falls dangerously ill. Before and during actual conclaves it is next to impossible to lay your hands on a copy. Peter Bander's interpretations, filled as they are with the highly condensed soup of scholarship as well as with the lightning flashes of nearly pure inspiration, should soon be recognized as *the* authoritative version and will doubtless be in sharp demand.

Which makes me admire all the more the modesty of Peter Bander, who, having forged such a masterwork of authenticity can then step humbly aside and say, as he does in his introduction, that the reader need not "extend to them the same reverence you may extend to the Gospels".

Reverence no; but profound respect, certainly. Only once did the author strain my credulity and that so slightly as to be virtually insignificant. He circulates the rumor that during the conclave which was to elect John XXIII, a certain Cardinal from the United States, evidently having taken Malachy's forecast that the next pope would be "pastor and mariner" literally, rented a boat, filled it with sheep and sailed thus conspicuously up and down the Tiber. Pope John, of course, as bishop of Venice, had the maritime claim nailed down.

What disturbs me and should disturb the reader to an equal degree is that after "Flower of Flowers", that is to say after Paul VI, there are only three more prophecies. Whoever he turns out to be, *Petrus Romanus* will be the last. Time is running out. It's later than we all think. The end of the world is at hand. If Malachy and Peter Bander say it's going to happen, then happen it surely will.

FOREWORD

In publishing THE PROPHECIES OF ST. MALACHY Colin Smythe Limited have produced an instructive and entertaining book.

There is a great deal of instant information in Peter Bander's nutshell biographical accounts of the popes who occupied the Roman See since the year 1143 to our present time—and indeed of the antipopes as well. The remarkable way in which the visions St. Malachy is alleged to have had are shown to apply to the successive individual popes is most amusing. Is it not the case to repeat: "Se non è vero, è ben trovato"?

Whatever one may think of the genuineness of the prophecies attributed to St. Malachy, here is a fascinating study which provides the curious reader with much profit and pleasure.

ARCHBISHOP H. E. CARDINALE

Apostolic Nuncio to Belgium, Luxembourg, and the E.E.C.

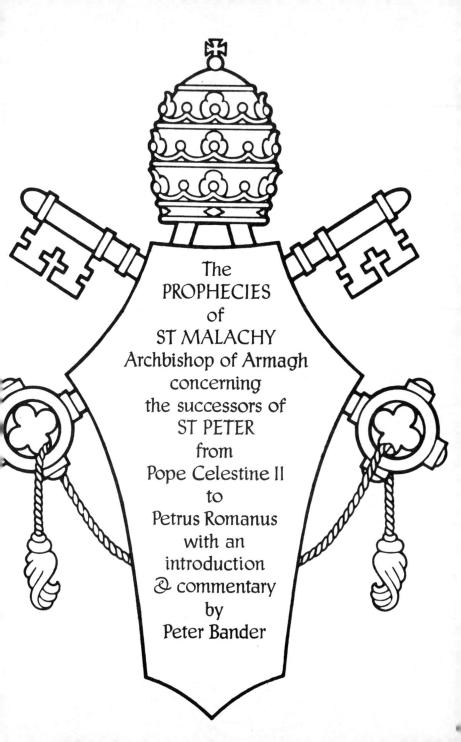

The
PROPHECIES
of
ST MALACHY
Archbishop of Armagh
concerning
the successors of
ST PETER
from
Pope Celestine II
to
Petrus Romanus
with an
introduction
& commentary
by
Peter Bander

THE PROPHECIES OF MALACHY

The prophecies of St. Malachy have almost come to an end; just one more pope, *Gloria Olivae*, and the one hundred and eight popes prophesied by St. Malachy with short Latin descriptions will have become part of history. Only once more will punters use the Malachy Prophecies to speculate on a papal election; only one more time will interpreters of Malachy try to make facts fit the prophecies. The Benedictine historian Arnold Wion was the first to mention these prophecies in his book *Lignum Vitæ*, published in 1559. With the briefest of introductions he inserted them after an equally brief summary of St Malachy's life. Since then a never ending controversy about the authenticity and authorship of the prophecies has led to many new editions and publications of the same, each trying to prove the author's personal belief. In the seventeenth century Father Menestrier, a famous Jesuit, put forward his hypothesis that these prophecies had originated in 1590 during the conclave which resulted in Gregory XIV becoming the elected pontiff. Fr. Menestrier goes as far as naming the forger; a member of Cardinal Simoncelli's party is supposed to have forged these prophecies in order to influence the electors in favour of his Cardinal who was the doyen of the Sacred College and, by virtue of his office and other qualities, surely a favourite for the pontificate. Cardinal Simoncelli was Bishop of Orvieto, his birthplace, and the motto given to him in the prophecies, *Ex antiquitate urbis*, is simply an allusion to Orvieto (*Latin: Urbs vetus*). Perhaps it is fair to add that Fr. Menestrier does not furnish us with evidence to substantiate his accusation. In 1871 Abbé Cucherat put forward his hypothesis; Malachy had his visions between the end of 1139 and the beginning of 1140 during his visit to Rome. He committed the visions to paper and handed the manuscript to Pope Innocent II to comfort the Holy Father in his afflictions. Innocent II placed the manuscript in the archives where they remained unread for nearly four centuries. Unfortunately Abbé Cucherat does not supply his evidence

9

either. If we were to place the works of those who have repudiated the Prophecies of Malachy on scales and balance them against those who have accepted them, we would probably reach a fair equilibrium; however, the most important factor, namely the popularity of the prophecies, particularly among the ordinary people (as distinct from scholars), makes them as relevant to the second half of the twentieth century as they have ever been. St Malachy's family name was O'Morgair and he was born in Armagh, Ireland, in 1094, almost one thousand years ago. He was baptised in Maelmhaedhoc (this name has been Latinized as Malachy) and he studied under Imhar O'Hagan who later became the Abbot of Armagh. In 1119 he was ordained priest by St Cellach (Celsus), studied under St Malchus and in 1123 he was elected Abbot of Bangor. His spectacular career had not ended; a year later he was consecrated Bishop of Connor and in 1132 he became Primate of Armagh. However, owing to intrigues, he had to wait two years before he could finally take posesssion of the See of Armagh; even then he had to purchase the Bachal Isu (staff of Jesus) from Niall, the usurping lay-primate. He died in 1148 at Clairvaux in the arms of St Bernard.

Unlike the life of many saints, that of St Malachy is well documented because his contemporary, St Bernard of Clairvaux, acted as his biographer at the request of the Abbot of Mellifont.

St Bernard describes Malachy as distinguished for his meekness, humility, obedience, modesty and as truly diligent in his studies. He also tells us at length of Malachy foretelling the day and hour of his death. The Breviary in its office for the festival of St Malachy mentions that he was enriched with the gift of prophecy.

The interested reader who wishes to study the life of St Malachy in greater depth and detail may wish to read any of the numerous life stories which have been written. In the second half of the last century Malachy's prophecies concerning the popes were widely read and studied in Ireland; it is therefore not surprising to find some detailed accounts of the Saint's life written in those years.

Since St Malachy left his prophecies concerning the popes of the Catholic Church behind, some 900 years ago, there have been many interpreters and probably as many critics who have in their own way tried to make these prophecies palatable to the reader or denounce them as forgeries.

Two objections to the prophecies most critics have in common are first, the silence of St Bernard on the subject, and secondly the tortuous methods employed by some of Malachy's interpreters in applying the various prophecies to certain popes.

The fact that St Bernard of Clairvaux does not refer to the prophecies and catalogue them among Malachy's other writings simply confirms to me that his character assessment of the Saint which describes Malachy as humble, meek and modest, was true to form.

Bearing in mind the nature of Malachy's prophecies, one sees soon that they do not conform to the pattern of Old and New Testament prophecies; they are not warnings of imminent dangers or threats to mankind; they do not point to any actual disaster (not really, because the destruction of Rome is 112 Popes ahead of his time!). There is no guidance, just a monotonous litany of Latin words or phrases, each symbolising a successive pope.

The second criticism against Malachy's vision concerns the tortuous methods adopted by some interpreters in applying them to some of the Popes. In the case of Clement XI (1700-1721) to whom Malachy had given the motto *Flores circumdati* (surrounded with flowers), his followers even struck a medal during his reign which bore this motto. After all, Malachy's prophecies have been publicly known since 1559 and it is reasonable to assume that those who designed the medal knew of them.

However, it is fair to say that the vast majority of Malachy's predictions about successive Popes is amazingly accurate — always remembering that he gives only a minimum of information.

The first three pontiffs mentioned in his vision, *Ex castro Tiberis*, *Inimicus expulsus* and *Ex magnitudine montis* were Celestine II, Lucius II and Eugene III; their respective reigns, 1143-1144, 1144-1145 and 1145-1153 fell within the life time of Malachy.

Circumstantial evidence points, therefore, to a time before 1143 when Malachy had his visions. His visit to Pope Innocent II in 1139 appears to have resulted in unfulfilled requests; the Pope refused to grant Malachy permission to spend the remainder of his life at the monastery of Clairvaux; he promised to grant Malachy the Pallium for the diocese of Armagh and Tuam (a See lately erected by Celsus) but failed to keep his promise.

Perhaps it was Malachy's preoccupation with the Papacy, that sparked off his visions. Who knows? Perhaps he was given the privilege of seeing before him the long line of popes to come, the timelessness of his Church, the strife and struggle during the period of antipopes, until finally Petrus Romanus will reign and feed his flock amid tribulations.

Some interpreters have suggested that Malachy does not specifically mention that no other pope would reign between *Gloria olivæ* (no. 111) and *Petrus Romanus,* who will be the last (given as no. 112); they suppose that Malachy just gave the next one thousand years and then mentioned the last pope to bring his prophecies to a conclusion. Far be it from me to join them in their speculations.

We have now reached *Flos florum;* Pope Paul VI has indeed *Flos florum,* the Fleur-de-Lis in his coat of arms. Out of 92 popes whose arms are published by the Vatican, Pope Paul VI is the thirteenth with such a bearing. In some cases there appears to be a discrepancy between the arms published by the Vatican and those given by Panvinio. Those coats of arms published by the Vatican and reproduced in this book are of course the papal crests; Panvinio tends to refer to the family coat of arms of the particular pope. These two are often quite different and bear no relation to one another. For example Clement IV, described by Malachy as *Draco depressus* (The dragon crushed) is given a coat of arms with six Fleurs-de-Lis; Panvinio describes his arms as an 'eagle clawing a dragon', which is almost tailor-made for the prophecy.

I have always refused to be drawn into any speculations and interpretations concerning those predictions that had still to be fulfilled. When I began my work as editor of the prophecies, *De medietate lunae, De labore solis* and *Gloria olivae* were still to come. Although I was only in my thirties at that time, I wondered whether *De labore solis* would reign in my own lifetime. I was particularly interested in this prophecy because in 1856 one interpreter, who signed himself 'a son of St. Jarbath', was not quite sure how to translate the Latin legend;

he was dissatisfied with previous translations and opted for a new, though not original prophetic interpretation. He quoted from St. Matthew's Gospel *XXIV* (29): *The sun shall be darkened and the moon shall not give her light.* Somehow I found it difficult to envisage any more popes in Rome once Jesus's prophecies about the end of the world had come true. What about *Gloria olivae* and *Petrus Romanus*? I opted for the less dramatic interpretation of an armorial bearing. But I still caused embarrassment to one friend whose archiepiscopal arms featured the blazing sun. Although I am sure that he is destined for still higher office, my allusion to *De labore solis* turned out to be far off the mark.

Prophecies are predictions of future events which cannot be foreseen. I doubt anyhow whether many prophecies can be correctly interpreted by contemporaries of the prophet or before they come true. I even doubt that those who believe that they are experiencing the fulfilment of a prophecy are detached enough for a valid judgement. Explaining an armorial bearing presents no problem, but assessing world events with two or three Latin words is a different matter. Perhaps *De medietate lunae* is borne out by my interpretation, but the true meaning of *De labore solis* may still lie in the future.

We have one comfort: experience has shown that the Holy Ghost tends to work in spite of our meddling in all possible matters, and also quite independently of prophecies and interpreters; He even is known to have worked in the conclave in spite of heavy opposition from Princes of the Church. It is therefore reasonable to assume that if the Holy Ghost who inspired St Malachy is the same one who inspires the electors, he would fulfil the prophecies as well.

One of the strong objections against the prophecies of Malachy in certain Catholic circles appears to be the fact that among the successive popes mentioned, appear the references to the antipopes. Although two of them are clearly marked as schismatic, *Corvus Schismaticus* — the schismatic crow, and *Schisma Barchinonicum* — (he was a Canon of Barcelona), the others take their place among the legitimate popes without any special mention of their peculiar position.

I consider those objections quite unreasonable from people who accept that Judas Iscariot was one of the Apostles of Jesus and do not object to the many biblical characters who were called but never chosen. After all, these antipopes are historical characters, they all held high episcopal offices before claiming the supreme title to the See of St Peter and, they were, within limits, accepted as real popes by a large section of Catholic followers; the fact that events proved them wrong or even schismatic does not belittle the important function and position they commanded at the time. Giacconius, who in his commentary on Malachy's prophecies only lists the canonically elected popes, quarrels with Panvinio for ranking popes and antipopes next to one another. This great Schism in the Catholic Church, when popes and antipopes existed side by side, lasted for almost three centuries. St Antonius himself comments on this and points out that much is written by different parties in defence of the one or the other ecclesiastical dignitary. All sides were well defended by excellent theologians and Canon Lawyers, and in the end, the argument was settled by establishing the rightful successor of St Peter as the one who was canonically elected to the supreme office. St Antonius goes further by saying that the ordinary people could not possibly participate in such difficult and delicate discussion as they did not understand Canon Law; they followed the advice and guidance of their spiritual fathers and superiors. Personally, I consider the fact that antipopes are included in the list as a point in favour of Malachy.

Finally, the language of Malachy. Many a critic has commented on the use of Latin — or should I say the misuse of Latin by Malachy. This also has been brought into the argument about the authenticity of the prophecies. There are many different translations of the Latin descriptions, often confusingly different. For example, the scholar whom I mentioned before and who signs himself a 'son of St Jarbath', relies heavily on Wion; he translates *De schola exiet* (Pope Clement III, 1187-1191): "he shall go forth from the school". The Revd. Ailbe J. Luddy, O.Cist., in his excellent book *Life of Malachy,* translates the same phrase: "he will come out of a school". Such examples occur time and time again and it becomes obvious, even to the person who can speak little or no Latin, that in its original usage only one meaning could have been implied. However, one cannot entirely rule out the possibility of ambiguity by the writer of the prophecies, although I am inclined to look for faults among the in-

14

terpreters; in a way it does not matter at all, Malachy will neither gain nor lose by a wrong translation or interpretation.

I have discussed the prophecies of Malachy with many friends, among them Bishops, Archbishops and high prelates of the Roman Catholic Church, the Church of England and the Church of Ireland. We have always enjoyed our conversations and the tremendous sense of humour emanating from them. With no disrespect to the Saint, we have laughed at our personal idiosyncrasies in making certain Latin verses fit certain eminent dignitaries we knew, but most of all, we have realised that we shall still have to wait some time before we really know whether St Malachy has once again foiled our speculations, or if, perchance, one of us has been right. My advice to the reader of the following comments on St Malachy's prophecies is simple: please, do not extend to them the same reverence you may extend to the Gospels, and remember that to err is human, but to err too often is foolish.

Although the theory that the prophecies of Malachy might be 16th century forgeries has been put forward from time to time, it is of particular interest that one of the most respectable and outstanding historians of the 16th century seems to have accepted them completely. Onofrio Panvinio, who had turned down episcopal honours, became correcter and reviser of the Vatican Library in 1556. Most interpreters of Malachy rely on his "Epitome Romanorum Pontificum" when commenting on the first sixty-nine popes on Malachy's list. This book was written in the reign of Pope Paul IV.

It is of interest to observe that the order of succession, particularly where the antipopes are concerned, has always been subject to editorial activity. I have started with the premise that the prophecies of Malachy concern the successors of St Peter in the Roman Catholic Church; the only legitimate order is therefore the one which is canonically correct. In the annual Vatican year book is a section: "Serie dei Sommi Pontefici Romani", which I have used with the kind permission of His Excellency the Apostolic Delegate to the United Kingdom. However, this has presented me with one problem: mention is made in the official list issued by the Vatican of an antipope INNOCENT III (di Sezze; Lando, 29.ix.1179-1180); this antipope does not appear in any of the commentaries on Malachy's prophecies. On the other hand, no mention is made in the official list of the antipope Clement VIII (1424-1429) whom, as I mentioned earlier, Panvinio ranks among the legitimate Popes of Rome. This is strange, and I have no explanation to offer. Among the 112 popes mentioned by Malachy are ten antipopes who all fall into the period between Alexander III (1159) and Nicolas V (1447). This alone makes the theory that the prophecies originated in the 16th century unlikely. References by previous interpreters concerning armorial bearings of popes before the latter part of the 12th century must be considered with caution because heraldic devices were not evident before that time. Papal armorial bearings, which we have reproduced from the same year book (Serie dei Sommi Pontefici) begin with the coat of arms of Pope Innocent III (1198-1216). The dates of election and accession to the See of St Peter are those officially recorded by the Vatican. Where there are more than one translation from Malachy's original Latin description, I have given those most commonly used in earlier commentaries.

In my commentary on Malachy's prophecies I have made extensive use of the early interpretations and those of the 19th century. These, however, finish with *Crux de Cruce* (PIUS IX), and I have attempted to complete the interpretations up to *Flos Florum* (PAUL VI) on similar lines as those followed earlier.

For the reader's benefit I have added a brief "curriculum vitæ" of the popes mentioned by Malachy. For references I have used "I SOMMI PONTEFICI ROMANI" (Vatican 1968) and THE CATHOLIC ENCYCLOPEDIA (New York). The papal coats of arms are reproduced from 'STEMMI DEI SOMMI PONTEFICI (Vatican 1968).

I wish to emphasise that my comments on the three prophecies yet to be fulfilled are pure guesses on my part and I beg the Dean and the College of Cardinals who will elect the future popes, not to be unduly influenced by my descriptions. I am sure that those eminent gentlemen whom my guess might fit, will forgive me for appearing to be canvassing. Finally, I wish to reiterate what I have said earlier, the final decision as to who is going to be the next pope and his successors, rests with the Holy Spirit.

STEMMI DEI SOMMI PONTEFICI

DAL SEC. XII AD OGGI

INNOCENZO III 1198 — 1216 LOTARIO DEI CONTI DI SEGNI	**ONORIO III** 1216 — 1227 CENCIO SAVELLI	**GREGORIO IX** 1227 — 1241 UGOLINO DEI CONTI DI SEGNI	**CELESTINO IV** 1241 — 1241 GOFFREDO CASTIGLIONI
INNOCENZO IV 1243 — 1254 SINIBALDO FIESCHI	**ALESSANDRO IV** 1254 — 1261 RINALDO DEI CONTI DI SEGNI	**URBANO IV** 1261 — 1264 GIACOMO PANTALÉON	**CLEMENTE IV** 1265 — 1268 GUIDO FOULQUOIS
B. GREGORIO X 1271 — 1276 TEBALDO VISCONTI	**B. INNOCENZO V** 1276 — 1276 PIETRO DI TARANTASIA	**ADRIANO V** 1276 — 1276 OTTOBONO FIESCHI	**GIOVANNI XXI** 1276 — 1277 PIETRO IULIANI
NICCOLÒ III 1277 — 1280 GIOVANNI GAETANO ORSINI	**MARTINO IV** 1281 — 1285 SIMONE DE BRION	**ONORIO IV** 1285 — 1287 GIACOMO SAVELLI	**NICCOLÒ IV** 1288 — 1292 GIROLAMO MASCI

17

CELESTINE II
1143 - 1144

GUIDO DE CASTELLO

Guido de Castello was a native of Roman Tuscany whose date of birth is unknown. He died on the 8th March 1144. He was made Cardinal in 1128, in 1140 he was made Papal Legate to France where he incurred the displeasure of St Bernard for the protection accorded by him to Arnold of Brescia. He succeeded Innocent II on the 25th September 1143 and at once lifted from France the interdict that his predecessor had inflicted because of the act of Louis VII in opposing his own candidate to the rightfully elected Bishop of Bourges. On the eve of a serious conflict with Roger of Sicily, Celestine II died, after a short reign of about six months.

Malachy's prophecy is a reference to the Pope's family name.

INIMICUS EXPULSUS
The enemy expelled

LUCIUS II
1144 - 1145

GERARDO CACCIANEMICI

Gerardo was born in Bologna (date unknown) and he died in Rome on the 15th February 1145. Before entering the Roman Curia he was a Canon in Bologna. In 1124 he was created Cardinal Priest and from 1125 to 1126 he was Papal Legate in Germany. During the pontificate of Innocent II we find Gerardo three times as Legate in Germany, and it was largely due to him that King Lothiar III made two expeditions to Italy for the purpose of protecting Innocent II against the antipope Anacletus II. Towards the end of the pontificate of Innocent II he was appointed Papal Counsellor and Librarian. On the 12th March 1144 he was elected and consecrated Pope. His reign was a troubled one and if we can believe the statement of Godfrey de Viterbo in his *Pantheon*, Lucius II marched upon the Capitol at the head of a small army where he suffered defeat and was severely injured by stones that were thrown upon him on this occasion and which caused his death a few days later. During his reign he was especially well disposed towards the order of the Premonstratensians.

Malachy's description *Inimicus expulsus* appears to be an allusion to the Pope's family name. We have already stated what his family name was; *Cacciare* in Italian means to expel and *nemici* are the enemies.

EX MAGNITUDINE MONTIS
From the great mountain

EUGENE III
1145 - 1153

BERNARDO FORSE DEI PAGANELLI DI MONTEMAGNO

Bernardo was elected Pope on the 15th February 1145, and died in Tivoli on the 8th July 1153. On the same day that Pope Lucius died, the Sacred College foreseeing that the Roman populace would make a determined effort to force the new Pope to abdicate his temporal power, withdrew to the remote cloisters of St Caesarius and elected a candidate outside their body. They chose, unanimously, the Cistercian monk Bernard of Pisa, Abbot of the monastery of Tre

Fontane. He was enthroned as Eugene III without delay, and since residence in the rebellious city was impossible, the Pope and his Cardinals fled to the country. St Bernard received the news of the elevation of his disciple with astonishment and pleasure and wrote to the new Pope a letter containing the famous and often quoted passage — "Who will grant me to see, before I die, the Church of God as in the days of old, when the apostles laid down their nets for a draught, not of silver and gold, but of souls?" Eugene is said to have gained the affection of the people by his affability and generosity. During his lifetime he continued to wear the coarse habit of Clairveaux beneath the purple and the virtues of monasticism accompanied him through his stormy career. St Antoninus described Eugene III as one of the greatest and most afflicted Popes.

Malachy's *ex magnitudine montis* refers to his place of birth, Montemagno.

ABBAS SUBURRANUS
Abbot from Suburra

ANASTASIUS IV
1153 - 1154

CORRADO

Corrado was crowned Pope on the 12th July 1153 and died in Rome on the 3rd December of the following year. He is chiefly known for his attitude towards Frederick Barbarossa and his recognition of Wichmann as Bishop of Magdeburg. Interpreters of Malachy differ in their explanation of the word *Suburranus*. Some refer to his birthplace, which is said to have been a locality called *Suburra,* others maintain that *Suburranus* is used in reference to one steering a great vessel.

DE RURE ALBO

(a) From a white country
(b) Of the Alban country

ADRIAN IV
1154 - 1159

NICHOLAS BREAKSPEAR

Little is known about the parentage or boyhood of Adrian although it is recorded that he was probably born in Abbots Langley, Hertfordshire. Adrian went abroad as a poor wandering scholar and begged his way to the famous university of Paris. He was admitted among the regular canons of St Rufus, where he was successively raised to the office of Prior and Abbot. However, the canons repented of their choice and appealed to the Pope on two occasions, bringing various charges against him. Pope Eugene ordered the canons to elect another Abbot and raised Adrian to the rank of Cardinal Bishop of Albano in 1146. He was sent as Papal Legate to the kingdoms of Denmark, Sweden and Norway. On his return to Rome he was hailed the Apostle of the North and as the death of Anastasius IV occurred at that time on 2nd December 1154, Adrian was unanimously elected the successor of St Peter on the following day. The turbulent and fickle population of Rome was once again in open revolt under the leadership of Arnold of Brescia. King William of Sicily also showed open hostility and the professed friendship of Frederick Barbarossa was even more dangerous. When Cardinal Gerardo was mortally wounded in broad daylight, Adrian at once laid the city under an interdict and retired to Viterbo. He forbade the observance of any sacred service until the Wednesday of Holy Week and the Senators were impelled to prostrate themselves before His Holiness. Submission was made and the ban removed. In June 1155 the famous meeting between Frederick of Hohenstauffen, then the most powerful ruler in Europe, and Adrian, the most powerful spiritual leader in the world, took place about thirty miles north of Rome. This ultimately led to the crowning of Frederick in St Peter's. In 1156 Adrian collected his vassals and mercenaries and marched south to Beneventum where he remained until June 1156. It was during this time that John of Salisbury spent three months with him and obtained from the Pope the famous Donation of Ireland. In his work *Metalogicus* John records, "At my solicitation (ad preces meas) he (Adrian IV) granted Ireland to Henry II, the illustrious King of England, to hold by hereditary right, as his letter to this day testifies. For all Ireland of ancient right, according to the Donation of Constantine, was said to belong to the Roman Church which he founded. He also sent by me a ring of gold, with the best of emeralds therein, wherewith the investiture might be made for his governorship of Ireland, and that same ring was ordered to be and is still in the public treasury of the king."

The suggestion that because he was born in England Adrian made Ireland over to King Henry II, who was no relation of his, does not merit serious attention. The only objection raised to John of Salisbury's statement is that it may be an interpolation. If it is not an interpolation it constitutes a complete proof of the donation, the investiture by the ring being legally sufficient. The Pope's Bull known as *Laudabiliter* does not purport to confer Ireland by hereditary right, but the letter referred to was not the Bull but a formal letter of investiture. The overwhelming weight of authority is in favour of the genuineness of the passage in *Metalogicus*. The Bull *Laudabiliter* has often been considered doubtful. Assuming the statements in *Metalogicus* to be correct, the text relating to the donation of Adrian may be arranged as follows : —

(1) The letter of investiture referred to by John of Salisbury, 1156.

(2) *Laudabiliter*, prepared in 1156 and issued in 1159,

(3) A confirmation of the letter of investiture by Alexander III in 1159.

(4) Three letters of Alexander III in 1172 which confirm *Laudabiliter*.

The Bull was not sent forward in 1156, because the offer of Adrian was not then acted on, but the investiture was accepted. At a council held in Winchester on the 29th September 1156 the question of subduing Ireland and giving it to William, Henry's brother, was considered, but the expedition was put off to another time.

The donation of Adrian was subsequently recognised in many official writings, and the Pope, for more than four centuries, claimed the overlordship of Ireland.

Pope Adrian IV died at Anagni in open strife with the Emperor Frederick Barbarossa who was in league with the Lombards against him. Alexander III carried out the intentions of Adrian and shortly afterwards excommunicated the Emperor.

Malachy's prophecy *de rure albo* appears to be most appropriate. Adrian was born in England, which was called Albion on account of the white rocks and white cliffs. His birthplace was near the Abbey of St Albans and he was consecrated Cardinal Bishop of Albano. Last, but not least, he was hailed the Apostle of the North, where he had worked in countries of perpetual snow.

EX ANSERE CUSTODE
From the guardian goose

ALEXANDER III
1159 - 1181

ROLANDO BANDINELLI

Rolando Bandinelli was born of a distinguished Sienese family. He was a professor in Bologna and was called to Rome by Eugene III in the year 1150, where he soon became Cardinal of the title of St Mark and Papal Counsellor. After the death of Pope Adrian IV (1st September 1159), of the twenty-two Cardinals assembled to elect a successor all but three voted for Rolando. In opposition to Cardinal Rolando, who took the name of Alexander III, the three imperialist members of the conclave chose one of their own number, Cardinal Octavian, who assumed the title of Victor IV. The Emperor summoned both claimants before a packed assembly at Pavia where he addressed Octavian as Victor IV, and the canonically elected Pope as Cardinal Rolando. Pope Alexander refused to submit his clear right to this tribunal, which, as was foreseen, declared for the usurper on the 11th February 1160. Alexander promptly responded by excommunicating the Emperor and releasing his subjects from their oaths of allegiance. The ensuing schism was far more disastrous to the empire than to the papacy. It lasted for seventeen years and only ended after the battle of Legnano in 1176, with the unconditional surrender of Barbarossa, in Venice, in 1177. Alexander's enforced exile in France 1162 to 1165) helped greatly to enhance the dignity of the papacy, never so popular as when in distress. It also brought him into direct contact with the most powerful monarch of the West, Henry II of England. After Thomas Becket's murder the Pope succeeded, without actual recourse to ban or interdict, in obtaining from the penitent monarch every right for which the martyr had died.

In 1179 Alexander convoked and presided over the third Lateran Council. At this council the exclusive right of papal elections was vested in a two-third majority of the Cardinals. Alexander III died on the 3rd August 1181.

Panvinio refers to Alexander as *de familia Paparona*. In Ciacconius' edition (1677) it is stated that he belonged to the noble family of "Bandinella" which was afterwards called Paparona. Referring to the Pope's family coat of arms, Ciacconius maintains that there was a goose in it. Another interpreter reminds the reader that the family of Alexander III descended from one of those who, aroused by geese, when Brennus attempted to sack the capital, repulsed him. In this particular case the entire evidence for Malachy appears to rest on the assumption that the family name of the Pope was Paparona. There seems to be an absolute definiteness about this in early interpretations. Panvinio, who is usually relied upon whenever a question of genealogy is raised, finds himself criticised by later interpreters for "chiming in with the prophecy". Abbé Cucherat explains the legend by a classic allusion to the honoured bird which saved Rome. According to him Malachy made a classic, as well as mystic, allusion to the salvation of Rome by Alexander III.

EX TETRO CARCERE
From the Loathsome Prison

V I C T O R   I V (ANTIPOPE)
1159 - 1164

OTTAVIANO MONTICELLO

Ottaviano was Cardinal of the title of St Nicholas at the Tullian prison. Panvinio gives him the same title, whilst others proclaim him to be Cardinal of St Sicilia. He was elected on the 7th September 1159 by a small minority of Cardinals, the clergy of St Peter and the Roman populace, while the majority of the College of Cardinals elected Cardinal Rolando who assumed the title of Alexander III. Ottaviano belonged to one of the most powerful Roman families (Count Tuscalan's) and had been a Cardinal since 1138. As he was considered a great friend of Barbarossa he rested his hopes on the Emperor backing his election to the Papal see. He died at Lucca on the 20th April 1164 and was succeeded by the antipope Paschal III.

Malachy's Latin description is an allusion to his Cardinal title.

VIA TRANSTIBERINA
The road beyond the Tiber

P A S C H A L   I I I (ANTIPOPE)
1164 - 1168

GUIDO DA CREMA

Via Transtiberina refers to St Mary's in Transtevere, which was the Cardinal title of Paschal III. He was elected in 1164 to succeed Cardinal Ottaviano. To meet the demands of Frederick Barbarossa he canonized Charlemagne in 1165, but this action was never ratified by the Church. He died in 1168. There appears to be a great confusion among interpreters of Malachy, because the said cardinal title is often given to the antipope Callixtus III. According to Ciacconius, Paschal III and Callixtus III, together with their dates, should change places, and the rest should be left to stand. Others maintain that Callixtus had no title in the city of Rome. So that the reader may be aware of this confusion I prefer to introduce the next antipope, Callixtus III, at this point, rather than be guilty of presenting an authoritative statement as to their respective Cardinal titles.

DE PANNONIA TUSCIÆ
From the Hungary of Tuscia

CALLIXTUS III
1168 - 29/8/1178*

GIOVANNI DI STRUMI

Callixtus III was the Hungarian John, Abbot of Struma.

Malachy's Latin legend for Paschal III and Callixtus III are obvious allusions to their ecclesiastical titles, which appear to be in dispute. However, historians are satisfied that Paschal was in fact Cardinal Bishop of St Mary in Transtevere and Callixtus was from Hungary.

At this point the *Serie dei Sommi Pontefici Romani* gives yet another antipope, Innocent III. His place of origin is Sezze, Lando, and his tenure of office is given as 1179 to 1180. There is no reference to Innocent III (the antipope) in Malachy or any of his interpreters. [See Clement VIII].

---

* date of his submission to Alexander III.

LUX IN OSTIO

(a) The light at the door.
(b) The light in Ostium
(c) A light in the gate

LUCIUS III

1181 - 1185

UBALDO ALLUCINGOLI

Ubaldo was born in Lucca and created Cardinal Priest in 1141. In 1159 he became Cardinal Bishop of Ostia. After the death of Alexander III he was elected Pope in Velletri where he was crowned. He was compelled to leave Rome in 1182, but returned the following year in an attempt to put an end to the continual dissensions of the Romans. However, his life was made so unbearable that he had to leave the city for a second time. Though the relations between Lucius III and the Emperor Frederick I were not openly hostile they were always strained. Lucius III did not yield to the Emperor and demanded that German Bishops, unlawfully appointed by the anti-popes during the pontificate of Alexander III, should be re-consecrated and retain their sees. He died at Verona on the 25th November 1185.

Malachy's description appears to be a play on the words Lucius or Lucca and Ostia.

SUS IN CRIBRO
A sow in a sieve

URBAN III

1185 - 1187

UBERTO OF THE NOBLE MILANESE FAMILY OF CRIVELLI

Uberto was created a Cardinal by Lucius III in 1182 and Archbishop of Milan in 1185. He was elected to succeed Lucius and crowned on 1st December 1185. Urban inherited from his predecessor a legacy of feud with the great Emperor Frederick Barbarossa and this was embittered by personal hostility, for at the sack of Milan in 1162 the Emperor had caused several of the Pope's relatives to be mutilated. He died at Ferrara on the 19th October 1187.

Malachy's description is an allusion to the Pope's family name, Crivelli: Crivelli in Italian means a sieve. In his *Epitome*, Panvinio gives the arms of the Pope and there is a distinct representation of a sieve on the shield and the supporters of the crest are two sows. Ciacconius only gives the sieve.

ENSIS LAURENTII
The sword of Lawrence

GREGORY VIII
1187

ALBERTO DE MORRA

This Pope had only a pontificate of one month and 27 days. The year 1187 witnessed the almost complete obliteration of Christianity in Palestine. The fall of the Holy City struck Europe and Urban III is said to have died of a broken heart on 20th October. The following day the Cardinals elected Cardinal Alberto, a Beneventan of noble family. He was created Cardinal in 1155 and given the title of San Lorenzo in Lucina in 1158. He died in Pisa on the 17th December 1187.

There are two possible allusions in the prophecies of Malachy: firstly, Gregory VIII had been Cardinal of St Lawrence, and secondly, his armorial bearing was a drawn sword.

DE SCHOLA EXIET
(a)   He shall go forth from the school
(b)   He will come out of a school
(c)   Departed from school

CLEMENT III
1187 - 1191

PAOLO SCOLARI

During the short space (1181-1188) which separated the pontificates of Alexander III and Innocent III, not less than five pontiffs occupied the Papal chair in swift succession. They were all veterans trained in the school of Alexander. Two days after Gregory VIII's death the Cardinal Bishop of Palestrina, Paolo Scolari, was elected to the See of St Peter. This was a popular choice for the Romans, because he was the first Roman to be thus elevated to the papacy since the rebellion in the days of Arnold of Brescia. From the beginning, Pope Clement III concentrated on the task of massing the forces of Christendom against the Saracens. He was the organiser of the Third Crusade. His death occurred on the 27th March 1191.

Malachy's legend is merely an allusion to his family name and is to be understood as foretelling that this Pope was to be one of the Scolari.

DE (EX) RURE BOVENSI
(a)   From the Bovensian Territory
(b)   From the cattle country
(c)   From the country of Bovis

CELESTINE III
1191 - 1198

GIACINTO BOBONE

Giacinto Bobone was born in 1106 and became the first of the Roman family of Orsini to ascend to the chair of St Peter. On 30th

March 1191, in his eighty-fifth year, he was elected to succeed Clement III after forty-seven years as a Cardinal. As he was only a Cardinal Deacon, he was ordained Priest on the 13th April, and consecrated Bishop the next day. The following day he anointed and crowned King Henry VI of Germany as Emperor. Pope Celestine III canonized St Malachy of Armagh.

Malachy's description refers once again to the Pope's family name.

COMES SIGNATUS
A signed Count (Conti-Segni)

INNOCENT III
1198 - 1216

Lotario dei Conti di Segni

Lotario was born in 1160 in Anagni, the son of Count Trasimund of Segni and a nephew of Clement III. He became an outstanding theologian and when he returned to Rome after the death of Alexander III he held various ecclesiastical offices during the reigns of successive popes. Pope Gregory VIII created him Cardinal Deacon of St George in 1190 and later Cardinal Priest. During the pontificate of Celestine III, who was a member of the Houses of Orsini, enemies of the Counts of Segni, he lived in retirement. After the Pope's death Lotario was elected Pope on the same day on which Celestine III died. He was only 37 years old. There was scarcely a country in Europe over which Innocent III did not in some way or other assert the supremacy which he claimed for the papacy. He was a zealous protector of the true faith and a strenuous opponent of heresy. His great political/ecclesiastical achievements brought the papacy to the zenith of its power. He died on the 16th June 1216 in Perugia.

Malachy's legend refers to the illustrious family of the Conti of which the Conti di Segni was a branch.

CANONICUS DE LATERE
(a) A Canon from the side
(b) Canon of Lateran

HONORIUS III
1216 - 1227

Cencio Savelli

Cencio Savelli was born in Rome and was for a time canon at the Church of Santa Maria Maggiore. He became Papal Chamberlain in 1188 and Cardinal Deacon of Santa Lucia in 1193. Under Pope Innocent III he became Cardinal Priest of St John and St Paul and was appointed tutor to the future Emperor Frederick II in 1197. On the 18th July 1216, nineteen cardinals assembled in Perugia, where Innocent had died two days previously. The Cardinals agreed to an election by compromise and Cardinal Ugolino of Ostia (afterwards Pope Gregory IX) and Cardinal Guido of Praeneste were empowered to appoint a new Pope. Cencio Savelli was chosen and consecrated in Perugia and crowned in Rome on the 31st August. Again this was a popular choice in Rome. Unlike his predecessor he was very advanced in age when acceding to the papal throne. Honorius III became the patron of three great orders. He approved the rule of St Dominic in his Bull *Religiosam Vitam* on the 22nd December 1216, and that of St Francis in his Bull *Solet Annuere* on the 29th November 1223. On the 13th January 1226 he approved the Carmelite order in his Bull *Ut Vivendi Normam*. It is remarkable that out of six saints who were canonized by Honorius III, four were English or Irish. He died at Rome on the 18th March 1227.

Malachy obviously refers to the fact that Cencio Savelli was a canon of St John Lateran.

AVIS OSTIENSIS

The Bird of Ostia

GREGORY IX

1227 - 1241

Ugolino, dei Conti di Segni

Ugolino was born in 1145 at Anagni. Educated at Paris and Bologna and appointed successively Papal Chaplain, Archpriest of St Peter and Cardinal Deacon in 1198. In May 1206 he succeeded Octavian as Cardinal Bishop of Ostia. Honorius III made him Plenipotentiary Legate in 1217 and on the 18th March 1227, after the death of Pope Honorius III, the Cardinals once again agreed upon an election by compromise. Two of the three Cardinal electors were Ugolino and Conrad of Urach. At first Conrad of Urach was elected, but he refused the tiara lest it might appear that he had elected himself. All the Cardinals unanimously elected Ugolino on the 19th March 1227. He was then more than eighty years old. When still Cardinal Bishop of Ostia, Gregory IX would often wear the dress of St Francis, walk about barefoot with him and his disciples and discuss theological matters with Francis. St Francis loved him as his father, and in a prophetic spirit used to address him as "the Bishop of the whole world and the father of all nations". He was also a devoted friend of St Dominic and promoted the interests of his order in many ways. St Clare and her order stood also under the protection of Gregory IX. He was a great patron of other religious orders with whose help he planned the conversion of Asia and Africa. For a time Gregory IX lived in hope that he might bring about a reunion of the Latin and Greek Churches. In 1232 the Patriarch of Constantinople acknowledged the Papal primacy, but Gregory failed, like many other popes before and after him, in his efforts to reunite the two churches.

During the 13 years of his pontificate he created fourteen Cardinals, many of whom were members of religious orders. He died on the 22nd August 1241 at Rome. The arms of Gregory IX show

32

an eagle and he was Cardinal Bishop of Ostia. This is the first allusion to armorial bearings which can now be used in evidence. [See *Stemmi dei Sommi Pontefici*].

LEO SABINUS
The Sabinian Lion

CELESTINE IV
1241

GOFFREDO CASTIGLIONI

This pope was a native of Milan and a nephew of Urban III. He was probably a Cistercian. He was made a Cardinal by Gregory IX and succeeded him on the 25th October 1241. His death occurred after a reign of only fifteen days.

Malachy's prophecy is an allusion to the Pope's armorial bearing which features a lion. He is also said to have been Cardinal Bishop of Sabina (Episcopus Cardinalis Satinus) which, of course, has nothing to do with the Church and Convent of Saint Sabina in Rome.

COMES LAURENTIUS
Count Laurence

INNOCENT IV
1243 - 1254

SINIBALDO FIESCHI (COUNT OF LAVAGNA)

Born of one of the noble families of Genoa, Fieschi became Cardinal Priest of St Laurence in Lucina in 1228. When Celestine IV had died, the excommunicated Emperor Frederick II was in possession of the states of the Church around Rome and attempted to intimidate the Cardinals into electing a Pope of his choice. The Cardinals fled to Anagni and voted for Sinibaldo Fieschi, who ascended the Papal throne as Innocent IV in June 1243, after an interregnum of one year, seven months and fifteen days.

Sinibaldo Fieschi was Cardinal of St Laurence and Malachy's prophecy is an obvious reference to this.

SIGNUM OSTIENSE
(a) A sign of Ostia
(b) The standard of Ostia

ALEXANDER IV
1254 - 1261

RINALDO DEI SIGNORI DI IENNE

Rinaldo was born of the noble house of Segni which had already given two sons to the Papacy, and was created Cardinal Bishop of Ostia by his uncle Gregory IX. On the death of Innocent IV in 1254, the aged Cardinal was unanimously chosen to succeed him. As Pope he showed great favour to the Order of St Francis and one of his first acts was to canonise St Clare. He died on the 25th May 1261.

Signum Ostiense is an enigmatic way of pointing to the Bishop being of the house of Conti-Segni and also Cardinal Bishop of Ostia.

HIERUSALEM CAMPANIÆ
Jerusalem of Champagne

URBAN IV
1261 - 1264

JACQUES PANTALEON

Jacques, the son of a French cobbler, was born in Troyes. After being a Canon and Archdeacon of Liège, he became Bishop of Verdun in 1254 and Patriarch of Jerusalem in 1255. After the death of Alexander IV he was elected Pope. He died on the 2nd October 1264.

Born in Champagne and raised to the title of Patriarch of Jerusalem, Malachy's description appears most appropriate.

DRACO DEPRESSUS
The dragon crushed

CLEMENT IV
1265 - 1268

GUIDO FULCODI

Guido was born in Saint-Gilles on the Rhone, and made a rapid rise in the Church. In 1261 he became Cardinal Bishop of Sabina and was elected Pope, against his will, on the 5th February 1265. He accepted this position with great reluctance. After his death in 1268 the Papal throne remained vacant for nearly three years.

Panvinio in his *Epitome* shows an eagle clawing a dragon. However, his official coat of arms shows six fleurs de lis. Abbé Cucherat explains the Latin Legend metaphorically by pointing out that Pope Clement IV crushed nepotism, which he describes as the dragon in the Church at that time. It is a well documented fact that his first act as Pope was to forbid any of his relatives to come to the Curia, or to attempt to derive any sort of temporai advantage from his elevation.

ANGUINEUS VIR
(a)   The man of the serpent
(b)   A snake-like man

GREGORY X
1271 - 1276

TEBALDO VISCONTI

Tebaldo Visconti was born in 1210 and became Archdeacon of Liège. After the death of Pope Clement IV the French and Italian Cardinals could not agree on a candidate. Three years later they voted for Tedaldo Visconti, who was not only not a Cardinal but not even a priest. He accepted the Papal dignity and took the name of Gregory X. From the very beginning of his pontificate Gregory sought to promote the interests of the Holy Land. He died on the 10th January 1276.

Again the coat of arms as given by Panvinio differs substantially from that which is attributed to him in later centuries. Panvinio quite plainly shows a serpent in the armorial bearings of the Pope and his family.

CONCIONATOR GALLUS
A French Preacher

INNOCENT V
1276

Petrus A Tarantasia

Born in 1225 in south eastern France, Tarantasia became Archbishop of Lyons in 1272 and Cardinal Bishop of Ostia in 1273. He was the intimate adviser of Gregory X whom he succeeded on the 21st January 1276. Thus he became the first Dominican Pope. He died in June 1276.

Malachy's prophecy refers to Innocent V having been a member of the order of Preachers, and a Frenchman.

BONUS COMES
A Good Count

ADRIAN V
1276

Ottobono Fieschi

This nephew of Innocent IV reigned only from the 12th July to the 21st August 1276. Adrian V was a count and his name Ottobono furnishes an explanation to the second half of the prophecy.

PISCATOR TUSCUS
A Tuscan Fisherman

JOHN XXI
1276 - 1277*

PIETRO JULIANI

Pietro was born in Lisbon. He was appointed Cardinal Bishop of Tusculum and in 1276 he was elected to succeed Adrian V. On the 14th May 1277 while the Pope was alone in his apartment, it collapsed and he was buried under the ruins.

Piscator obviously refers to his name Petrus; Tuscus is an adjective used (probably in error) to refer to Tusculum.

ROSA COMPOSITA
(a)   The Modest Rose   (b)   The Rose Composite

NICHOLAS III
1277 - 1280

GIOVANNI GAETANO ORSINI

Giovanni was born in Rome in 1216 of the the illustrious Roman family of Orsini. He was created Cardinal Deacon with a title of St Nicholas by Innocent IV. After the death of John XXI he succeeded him as Pope in 1277.

Giovanni Gaetano Orsini bore a rose in his coat of arms.

---

* After John XIV had been removed by force, the usurper Boniface VII reigned eleven months, dying in July 985. A Roman named John was then elected Pope and crowned. Some historians, and even Papal catalogues, give as the immmediate successor to Boniface yet another John, who is supposed to have reigned for four months and is placed by a few historians in the list of Popes as John XV. Although this alleged Pope John never existed, the fact that he has been catalogued by these historians has thrown into disorder the enumeration of the Popes named John, the true John XV often being called John XVI. This confusion was remedied when Cardinal Roncalli took the name John XXIII, ascending to the throne of St Peter in 1958, nearly 1,000 years after the confusion started.

EX TELONIO LILIACEI MARTINI
(a) From the office of Martin of the lilies
(b) From the receipt of custom of Martin of the lilies

MARTIN IV
1281 - 1285

SIMONE DE BRION

Simone was born in the Castle of Montpensier in the old French province of Touraine, and became Canon and Treasurer at the Church of St Martin in Tours. King Louis IX made him Chancellor of France in 1260 and Urban VI created him a Cardinal. Six months after the death of Pope Nicholas III, Simone de Brion was unanimously elected Pope in 1281. He died on the 28th March 1285.

St Malachy obviously refers to the Pope's position as Treasurer of St Martin of Tours; the fleur-de-lis is a well known emblem of France.

EX ROSA LEONINA
From the leonine Rose

HONORIUS IV
1285 - 1287

GIACOMO SAVELLI

Giacomo Savelli, who was born in Rome in 1210 had, it seems, an unspectacular career before ascending to the Papal throne. In 1261 he was created Cardinal by Martin IV who also made him Captain of the Papal army. His election to the papacy was one of the speediest in history; three days after the death of Pope Martin IV fifteen out of the eighteen Cardinals who then composed the Sacred College

38

elected the Pope without the Conclave, which had been prescribed by Gregory X, but suspended by John XXI. At the first vote taken Giacomo Savelli was unanimously elected and took the name of Honorius IV. He died in Rome on the 3rd April 1287.

Malachy's description is an allusion to the Pope's coat of arms which shows two lions holding a rose.

PICUS INTER ESCAS
A woodpecker among the food

NICHOLAS IV
1288 - 1292

GIROLAMO MASCI

Pope Nicholas IV had entered the Franciscan order at an early age and was sent in 1272 as a delegate to Constantinople to invite the participation of the Greeks in the Second Council of Lyons. Two years later he succeeded St Bonaventure in the Generalship of his order. He was created a Cardinal in 1278 and Martin IV appointed him Bishop of Palestrina. After the death of Honorius IV on the 3rd April 1278 the Conclave was hopelessly divided in its election of a successor. It was not until the following year on the 15th February 1288 that the Cardinals unanimously elected Girolamo Masci. He died in Rome on the 4th April 1292.

Malachy's prophecy is most obscure. It has been suggested that *Picus inter escas* is an enigmatic allusion to the fact that Nicholas came from Ascoli in Picenum; however, this explanation appears to me to be too far fetched. On the other hand I have no better one to offer, as the records of the Pope's life are very sketchy.

The fact that Malachy's description makes little sense to us does not prove that it was meaningless at the time when it was made or when Nicholas IV became Pope.

S. CELESTINO V	BONIFACIO VIII	B. BENEDETTO XI	CLEMENTE V
1294 1294	1294 1303	1303 1304	1305 1314
PIETRO DEL MURRONE	BENEDETTO CAETANI	NICCOLÒ BOCCASINI	BERTRANDO DE GOT
GIOVANNI XXII	BENEDETTO XII	CLEMENTE VI	INNOCENZO VI
1316 1334	1334 1342	1342 1352	1352 1362
GIACOMO DUÈSE	GIACOMO FOURNIER	PIETRO ROGER	STEFANO AUBERT
B. URBANO V	GREGORIO XI	URBANO VI	BONIFACIO IX
1362 1370	1370 1378	1378 1389	1389 1404
GUGLIELMO DE GRIMOARD	PIETRO ROGER DE BEAUFORT	BARTOLOMEO PRIGNANO	PIETRO TOMACELLI
INNOCENZO VII	GREGORIO XII	CLEMENTE VII	BENEDETTO XIII
1404 1406	1406 1415	1378 antip. 1394	1394 antip. 1423
COSMA MIGLIORATI	ANGELO CORRER	ROBERTO DEI CONTI DEL GENEVOIS	PIETRO DE LUNA
ALESSANDRO V	GIOVANNI XXIII	MARTINO V	EUGENIO IV
1409 antip. 1410	1410 antip. 1415	1417 1431	1431 1447
PIETRO FILARGO	BALDASSARRE COSSA	ODDONE COLONNA	GABRIELE CONDULMER

EX EREMO CELSUS

(a)   Elevated from the desert
(b)   The lofty one from the desert

CELESTINE V

1294

PIETRO DI MURRONE

Pietro was born in 1215, and became a Benedictine at the age of 17. His love of solitude led him into the wilderness of Montemorrone and later into the wilderness of Mount Majella. He followed the example of John the Baptist and wore hair-cloth roughened with knots. A chain of iron was fastened around him every day except Sundays, and for long stretches of time he lived on bread and water. In July 1294 three Cardinals accompanied by a great multitude of monks ascended the mountain and announced that Pietro had been chosen Pope by a unanimous vote of the Sacred College. Two years and three months had elapsed since the death of Nicholas IV. Pietro heard of his elevation with tears, but after a brief prayer obeyed what seemed the clear voice of God. Owing to his inexperience of diplomatic matters the affairs of the Curia fell into extreme disorder and he looked upon affairs of state as wasting time that ought to be devoted to exercises of piety. Because he feared that his soul was in danger he proposed abdication. The question arose for the first time whether a Pope could resign. On the 13th December he summoned the Cardinals and announced his resignation and proclaimed the Cardinals free to proceed to a new election. He was most cruelly treated by his successor Boniface VIII, who had him arrested and imprisoned. He died in prison on 19th May 1296.

Malachy's prophecy appears to have been remarkably fulfilled.

EX UNDARUM BENEDICTIONE
From a blessing of the waves

BONIFACE VIII
1294 - 1303

BENEDETTO CAETANI

Born in 1235 in Rome, Benedetto was the son of a noble Spanish family which had established itself in Gaeta and later in Anagni. Through his mother he was related to the house of Segni. He obtained a doctorate in Canon and Civil Law and in 1265 he accompanied Cardinal Fieschi to England to restore harmony between Henry III and the rebellious barons. In 1276 he entered upon his career in the Curia where he soon acquired considerable influence. The abdication of Pope Celestine V has been frequently ascribed to the undue influence and pressure of Cardinal Caetani. It is probable that the elevation of this simple minded and inexperienced recluse did not commend itself to a man like Caetani, reputed to be the greatest jurist of his age and well skilled in the arts of Curial diplomacy. There can be no question that he treated his predecessor most cruelly. He entertained the most exalted notions on the subject of papal supremacy and was most emphatic in the assertion of his claims. His reign was marked by political intrigues all over the Western world in which he played no mean part. Reports that he died in a frenzy, gnawing his hands and beating his brains out against a wall, have never been proved. He died in Rome on the 11th October 1303.

The Latin legend of Malachy has been interpreted as referring to the Pope's armorial bearing, combined with the reference to his Christian name.

CONCIONATOR PATAREUS
A preacher from Patara

BENEDICT XI
1303 - 1304

Nicholas Boccasini

Nicholas was born in 1240 and entered the Dominican order at the age of fourteen. In 1296 he was elected Master General of the order. In this position he became one of the defenders of the unpopular Pontiff, who showed him many marks of favour and confidence. He became Bishop of Ostia and Dean of the Sacred College and when in 1303 the enemies of the Pope had made themselves masters of the Sacred Palace, only he and another Cardinal remained at the side of Boniface VIII to defend him. In October that year he was unanimously elected Pope. After a brief pontificate of eight months Benedict XI died suddenly. It was suspected that he had been poisoned.

Nicholas was a native of Patara and belonged to the Order of Preachers.

DE FESSIS AQUITANICIS
(a)   From the ditches of Aquitaine
(b)   From the Aquitanian fesses

CLEMENT V
1305 - 1314

Bertrand de Got

Bertrand de Got was born in France in 1264, of a distinguished family, his elder brother being the Archbishop of Lyons. He himself became Archbishop of Bordeaux. In 1305 after a Conclave of eleven months Bertrand de Got was elected Pope. During the usual Papal procession the Pope was thrown from his horse by a falling wall; one of his brothers was killed and so was Cardinal Matteo Orsini who had taken part in twelve Conclaves and seen thirteen Popes. The most precious jewel in the Papal crown was lost that day, an incident which has been prophetically interpreted by many. He died in April 1314.

Malachy's prophecy refers to the fact that the Pope came from Aquitania and makes heraldic reference to his armorial bearings.

DE SUTORE OSSEO
From the shoemaker of Osse

JOHN XXII
1316 - 1334

JACQUES DUESE

Jacques was born in 1249 and received his early education from the Dominicans. He became Bishop of Frejus in 1300 and Cardinal in 1312. After the death of Clement V the Papal See was vacant for two years and four months. In 1316 Jacques was chosen Pope. After his coronation at Lyons, John XXII moved to Avignon where he fixed his residence. He died on the 4th December 1334. His financial measures and centralisation of administration, and the fact that the transfer of the Papacy from Rome to Avignon had been made in the interests of France, made the Curia of Avignon generally detested. In fact the widespread distrust of the Papacy could not fail to result in consequences detrimental to the interior life of the Church.

Historians have always maintained that Jacques Duèse was the son of a shoemaker named Osse. If this is so, the legend is perfectly clear.

CORVUS SCHISMATICUS
A schismatical crow

NICHOLAS V (ANTIPOPE)
1328 - 1330

PIETRO RAINALLUCCI

In 1328 the excommunicated German King Louis of Bavaria received in Rome the Imperial Crown from Sciarra Colonna and on April 18th, and in the name of Louis of Bavaria, proclaimed John XXII a heretic, usurper and oppressor of the Church and also deprived him of his Papal dignities. A straw image of the Pope was publically burned in Rome and on the 12th May a Franciscan monk Pietro was proclaimed antipope by Louis, taking at his consecration the name of Nicholas V. In August 1330 Pietro wrote to Pope John XXII asking for pardon and absolution. This was granted; but Pietro was never allowed to leave the city where he spent the three remaining years of his life in voluntary penance and study. He died in 1333.

Medieval interpreters give this pope's name as Peter de Corberia or de Corbavio; the Vatican calender lists him as Pietro Rainallucci di Corvaro. Corvus appears an obvious allusion to the Pope's place of origin and Schismaticus places him among the ranks of the antipopes.

FRIGIDUS ABBAS
The cold Abbot

BENEDICT XII
1334 - 1342

JACQUES FOURNIER

Jacques was a Cistercian monk in the Monastery of Fontforide. The Abbot there was his uncle, Arnold Novelli, by whose name

Fournier was also known. He later became Abbot himself and was created Cardinal in 1310. He received the necessary two-thirds vote in December 1334 and was enthroned as Benedict XII on the 8th January 1335. He encountered much criticism and resentment and he died in Avignon in 1342.

Malachy's legend is explained by Panvinio's description "Abbas monasterii Fontis Frigidi".

EX ROSA ATRABENSIS
From the Rose of Arras

CLEMENT VI
1342 - 1352

PIERRE ROGER

Pierre Roger was born in 1291 in France and entered a Benedictine Monastery at the age of ten. He rapidly rose from one ecclesiastical dignity to another and he became Bishop of Arras and Chancellor of France in 1328. He was created a Cardinal in 1338 by Benedict XII whom he succeeded as Pontiff in 1342. During his reign he took up the long standing conflict between the Emperor Louis of Bavaria and the Papacy, and Louis finally submitted to the Pope. Clement was more a temporal prince than an ecclesaisitcal ruler; a patron of the arts, banquets and receptions to which ladies were freely admitted. The heavy expenses necessitated by such pomp soon exhausted the funds and Clement imposed an ever-increasing number of taxes, and appointments to Bishoprics were exclusively reserved for the Pope. He died after a short illness in December 1352 in Avignon.

Pierre Roger was Bishop of Arras, Episcopus Atrabensis, and his armorial bearings show six roses.

DE MONTIBUS PAMMACHII
From the mountains of Pammachius

INNOCENT VI
1352 - 1362

Stefano Aubert

Stefano Aubert was born in France, and began his career as Professor of Civil Law. His career in the Church was equally spectacular; in 1342 he became Cardinal Bishop. He was elected Pope at Avignon on the 18th December 1352, where he died on the 12th September 1362.

Malachy's prophecy refers to the fact that Innocent VI had been Cardinal Priest of Pammachius. Panvinio refers to his family crest showing six hills.

GALLUS VICECOMES
A French Viscount

URBAN V
1362 - 1370

Guglielmo de Grimoard

Guglielmo was born of a noble French family in 1310. He became a Benedictine monk and one of the greatest canonists of his day. In 1352 he became Abbot and started on a dipomatic career. Owing to jealousy within the Sacred College, which made the election of any one of its members impossible, Guglielmo De Grimoard was consecrated on the 6th November 1362 to succeed Innocent VI. He continued to wear the habit of the Benedictines. Urban was a patriotic Frenchman, which must be judged as a defect in the Pope of all Christendom; he estranged the English, aroused hostility in Italy and made many enemies. He died in Avignon on the 19th December 1370.

Malachy refers to the Pope's origin.

NOVUS DE VIRGINE FORTI
A new man from a strong virgin
[Motto also given as "Nova de virgine fortis]

GREGORY XI
1370 - 1378

PIERRE ROGER DE BEAUFORT

De Beaufort, born in 1331, was a nephew of Pope Clement VI who also created him Cardinal in 1348 when he was only eighteen years old. After the death of Urban V the Cardinals unanimously elected him Pope in Avignon in 1370. He died in 1378 in Rome.

Pierre Roger De Beaufort was Cardinal of the title of Santa Maria Nova and his name may be referred to in the word Forti. Another interpretation explains the legend as "renovated in spirit through the bold exhortation of the virgin Catherine of Siena".

DE INFERNO PREGNANI
(a) The Pregnani from hell
(b) From the hell of Pregnani

URBAN VI
1378 - 1389

BARTOLOMEO PRIGNANO

Bartolomeo was born in Naples in 1318. In 1364 he was consecrated Archbishop and after the death of Gregory XI the Conclave proposed him as candidate for the tiara. He became the first Roman Pope during the Western Schism in 1378. Urban VI is said to have died of poisoning in Rome on the 15th October 1389.

Malachy's legend is easily explained here: Urban VI was a Pregnani and a native of a place called Inferno near Naples.

CUBUS DE MIXTIONE
The square of mixture

BONIFACE IX
1389 - 1404

PIETRO TOMACELLI

Pietro who came from an ancient but impoverished noble family of Naples became the successor to the Roman Pope Urban VI on the 2nd November. The Avignon Pope, Clement VII, at the same time crowned the French Prince Louis of Anagni as King of Naples. He died in Rome on the 1st October 1404.

Malachy's prophecy is an allusion to the Pope's coat of arms, which had a bend chegny.

DE MELIORE SIDERE
From a better star

INNOCENT VII
1404 - 1406

COSMA MIGLIORATI

Born in 1336 Cosma became a Papal Delegate to England and in 1387 Archbishop of Ravenna. In 1389 Boniface IX created him Cardinal and on the 17th October 1404 he was elected Pope and took the name of Innocent VII. He died on the 6th November 1406. During his reign he did little for the suppression of the Schism.

Malachy's legend is both a play on words referring to the Pope's name and an allusion to his armorial bearings which show a comet.

NAUTA DE PONTE NIGRO
(a)   A sailor from a black bridge
(b)   The mariner of Negropont

GREGORY XII

1406 - 1415

ANGELO CORRER

Angelo Correr was born in 1327 in Venice. He became Bishop of Castello and Patriarch of Constantine in 1390. In 1405 he was made Cardinal and after the death of Innocent VII was elected Pope by the Cardinals in Rome on the 30th November 1406. Due to internal strifes Gregory XII resigned in 1415. The Cardinals accepted the resignation and appointed him Bishop of Porto. Two years later, before the election of a new Pope, Martin V, Gregory XII died.

Nauta appears to refer to Venice. Gregory XII was also Commendatarius of the Church of Nigripontis.

DE CRUCE APOSTOLICA
From the Apostolic Cross

CLEMENT VII (ANTIPOPE)

1378 - 1394

ROBERTO DEI CONTI DEL GENEVOIS

Cardinal of the title of the twelve apostles, this Pope's coat of arms shows a cross, quarterly pierced. He is responsible for the Great Schism of the West, a period in the history of the Church which lasted for nearly half a century.

LUNA COSMEDINA
The Moon of Cosmedin

BENEDICT XIII (ANTIPOPE)
1394 - 1423

PETER DE LUNA

This pope was the famous Peter De Luna, Cardinal of the title of St Mary in Cosmedina, who was born in 1328 and created Cardinal in 1375. He returned to Rome with Gregory XI after whose death he took part in the conclave which was attacked by the Romans and which elected Urban VI. His spiritual director and confessor was the great Vincent Ferrer, who believed him to be the real Pope. When Clement VII died he was unanimously chosen to succeed him. He died in Spain in 1423.

Malachy's description refers both to the antipope's name and his coat of arms.

SCHISMA BARCHINONICUM
The Schism of Barcelona

CLEMENT VIII (ANTIPOPE)
1423 - 1429

GIL SANCHEZ MUNOZ

This Pope is only recorded in a footnote to the Vatican list. However, Panvinio ranks him among the real Popes but adds "Sedit seu instrusus fuit". He was a Canon of Barcelona to which Malachy's description alludes and died in 1447.

[In the same footnote appears the name Bernardo Garnier who claimed the title Benedict XIV between 1425 and 1430.]

FLAGELLUM SOLIS
The lash of the sun

ALEXANDER V (ANTIPOPE)
1409 - 1410

PIETRO FILARGO

Pietro, born in 1339, was a homeless beggar boy in a Cretan city, knowing neither parents nor relations. He received elementary education from a friar and later entered a Franciscan monastery. Because of his unusual ability he was sent to be educated at Oxford and Paris where he distinguished himself as professor, preacher and writer. Pietro was made Bishop in 1386 and Pope Innocent VII made him a Cardinal in 1405. On the 26th June 1409 he was the unanimous choice of the Cardinals to fill the presumably vacant papal chair. His pontificate was marked by unsuccessful efforts to reach Rome. He died on 3rd May 1410 in Bologna, where he was held prisoner by Cardinal Cossa who succeeded Alexander V as John XXIII, on the 3rd May 1410.

CERVUS SIRENÆ
The Stag of the Syren

JOHN XXIII (ANTIPOPE)
1410 - 1415

BALDASSARRE COSSA

Baldassarre was born in 1370 and was one of the seven Cardinals who, in 1408, deserted Gregory XII and who had placed themselves under the jurisdiction of Benedict XIII. He became Cardinal in 1402 and Papal Legate in the following year. In 1409 Cossa played an important part in the Council of Pisa and when Popes Gregory XII and Benedict XIII were deposed, he conducted the election of Alexander V who remained entirely under his influence. He died on the 22nd November 1419.

Malachy's prophecy is an allusion to the fact that Cossa became Cardinal of the title of St Eustachius, who has the stag as an emblem. He was born in Naples which has the emblem of the syren.

COLUMNA VELI AUREI
The pillar with the golden veil

MARTIN V

1417 - 1431

ODDONE COLONNA

Oddone Colonna was born in 1368 and became a Papal Nuncio at various Italian courts under Boniface IX. In 1405 he was made a Cardinal (Velabro). He deserted Pope Gregory XII and participated in the election of the Antipopes Alexander V and John XXIII. The influential family of Colonna had already given twenty-seven Cardinals to the Church, but Martin V was the first to ascend to the Papal throne. The Church was just passing through the most critical period of its history, the great Western Schism. John XXIII had submitted to Pope Martin in 1419 and was given the title of Cardinal Bishop of Frascati. He died in Rome in 1431.

Malachy's prophecy is an allusion to the pope's cardinal title and his family name.

LUPA CŒLESTINA
The Cœlestinian she-wolf

EUGENE IV
1431 - 1447

GABRIELE CONDULMER

Gabriele was born at Venice in 1383 and was the nephew of Gregory XII. Although he inherited a vast fortune, he gave it away to the poor and entered a monastery. At the age of twenty-four he was appointed by his uncle as Bishop of Siena. In 1408 he was created Cardinal and became Pope in 1431. He died in Rome in 1447.

Malachy refers in his legend to the fact that Eugene IV belonged to the order of the Celestines and also was Bishop of Siena which bears a she-wolf on its arms.

AMATOR CRUCIS
A lover of the Cross

FELIX V (ANTIPOPE)
1439 - 1449

AMADEUS DUKE OF SAVOY

Amadeus was born in 1383. After the schismatic Council of Basle had declared the rightful pope, Eugene IV, deposed, the Cardinals wished to secure additional influence and financial support by turning to the rich and powerful Prince, the Duke Amadeus VIII of Savoy. After the death of his wife Maria of Burgundy, Duke Amadeus led a life of contemplation, in the company of five knights whom he had formed into the Order of St Maurice. He was consecrated and crowned by Cardinal d'Allamand in 1440. He submitted in 1449 to Nicholas V from whom he received the title of Cardinal of St Sabina. He died in 1451.

FELICE V 1439 1449 *antip.* AMEDEO DUCA DI SAVOIA	**NICCOLÒ V** 1447 1455 TOMMASO PARENTUCELLI	**CALLISTO III** 1455 1458 ALFONSO BORGIA	**PIO II** 1458 1464 ENEA SILVIO PICCOLOMINI
PAOLO II 1464 1471 PIETRO BARBO	**SISTO IV** 1471 1484 FRANCESCO DELLA ROVERE	**INNOCENZO VIII** 1484 1492 GIOVANNI BATTISTA CIBO	**ALESSANDRO VI** 1492 1503 RODRIGO BORGIA
PIO III 1503 1503 FRANCESCO TODE- SCHINI-PICCOLOMINI	**GIULIO II** 1503 1513 GIULIANO DELLA ROVERE	**LEONE X** 1513 1521 GIOVANNI DE' MEDICI	**ADRIANO VI** 1522 1523 ADRIANO FLORENSZ
CLEMENTE VII 1523 1534 GIULIO DE' MEDICI	**PAOLO III** 1534 1549 ALESSANDRO FARNESE	**GIULIO III** 1550 1555 GIOVANNI MARIA CIOCCHI DEL MONTE	**MARCELLO II** 1555 1555 MARCELLO CERVINI
PAOLO IV 1555 1559 GIAN PIETRO CARAFA	**PIO IV** 1559 1565 GIOVAN ANGELO DE' MEDICI	**S. PIO V** 1566 1572 ANTONIO (MICHELE) GHISLIERI	**GREGORIO XIII** 1572 1585 UGO BONCOMPAGNI

DE MODICITATE LUNÆ
From the littleness of the moon

NICHOLAS V
1447 - 1455

TOMMASO PARENTUCELLI

Tommaso was born in 1397 and acted as the factotum of the Bishop of Bologna for twenty years. He accompanied the Bishop on many missions and later became the protegé of Eugene IV who also entrusted him with other diplomatic tasks, which he carried out with such success that he received the Cardinal's hat in 1446. After the death of Pope Eugene, Parentucelli was elected Pope. He died in Rome in 1455.

Malachy's prophecy refers to his place of birth in the diocese of Luna and his humble origin.

BOS PASCENS
(a)   an ox feeding
(b)   a bull browsing

CALIXTUS III
1455 - 1458

ALFONSO BORGIA

Alfonso was born in 1378 of a noble family and after finishing his studies espoused the cause of Benedict XIII who created him a Canon. He submitted, however, to Martin V who appointed him Bishop of Valencia in 1429 and Eugene IV made him a Cardinal in 1444. In 1455 Alfonso de Borgia was elected Pope. His reign is remarkable for the revision of the trial of Joan of Arc, which was carried out by his directions and according to which the sentence of the first court was quashed and her innocence proclaimed. He was probably one of the richest Popes in history and died at Rome in 1458.

Malachy's prophecy is an allusion to the Pope's armorial bearing which shows the ox of the Borgias.

DE CAPRA ET ALBERGO
(Another version reads CUPRA)

PIUS II
1458 - 1464

ENEA SILVIO PICCOLOMINI

This pope was also born of a noble family, in 1405. He received elementary instruction from a priest and entered the University of Siena at the age of eighteen. He became the secretary to Bishop Capranica and later to the antipope Felix V. In 1445 he changed his allegiance and in 1447 became Bishop of Trieste. In 1456 he was created a Cardinal by Calixtus III whom he succeeded as Pope in 1458. He died on the 14th August 1464.

Malachy's description has been interpreted as being an allusion to the fact that Pius II had been secretary to Cardinal Capranica and Cardinal Albergato before he was elected Pope.

DE CERVO ET LEONE
From a stag and a lion

PAUL II
1464 - 1471

PIETRO BARBO

Pietro Barbo, a nephew of Eugene IV, was born in Venice in 1417 and entered the religious profession at the elevation of his uncle to the papacy. He was first Bishop of Cervia and Cardinal of Venice. He succeeded Pius II as Pope in 1464 and died in 1471.

Malachy refers to his Bishopric Cervia (stag) and his Cardinal title of St Mark (lion).

PISCATOR MINORITA
The Minorite Fisherman

SIXTUS IV
1471 - 1484

FRANCESCO DELLA ROVERE

Francesco was born in 1414. As a child he was placed in a Franciscan monastery because of the poverty of his parents. After filling the post of Procurator of his order in Rome, he was in 1467 created Cardinal by Paul II. He was elected Pope in 1471. His reign was overshadowed by political strifes and quarrels in which members of his family played leading parts and his appointing of men such as Pietro and Girolamo Riario to the highest offices in the Church are blots on his high office. He died in 1484.

Francesco was born the son of a fisherman and a member of the Minor Friars. [It is interesting to note that at the time of Malachy this Order did exist.]

PRÆCURSOR SICILIÆ
(a)   The Precursor of Sicily
(b)   The forerunner from Sicily

INNOCENT VIII
1484 - 1492

GIOVANNI BATTISTA CIBO

Giovanni was born in 1432 and entered the service of the Church after a somewhat licentious youth. In 1467 he became Bishop and in 1484 the successor to Sixtus IV. Great insecurity reigned at Rome during his rule, largely owing to weakness on his part in dealing with transgressors. In 1484 he issued his much abused Bull against witchcraft. Constantly confronted with financial difficulties he resorted to the objectionable habit of creating new offices and granting them to the highest bidders. A great number of Papal Bulls were sold during his reign, many of which are considered to be forgeries: among these latter must be placed the permission granted to the Norwegians to celebrate Mass without wine.

The only explanation Malachy's interpretors can give is that he spent much time at the court of the King of Sicily. Other explanations appear somewhat far-fetched, such as that the forerunner (Precursor) of Jesus was called John the Baptist which happened to be also the Pope's name.

BOS ALBANUS IN PORTU
The Alban bull at the port

ALEXANDER VI
1492 - 1503

RODRIGO BORGIA

The young Rodrigo who was born in Spain on the 1st January 1431, had not yet chosen his profession when the elevation of his uncle to the Papacy (1455) opened up new prospects to his ambition. His uncle conferred upon him rich benefices and sent him to study law at the University of Bologna. In 1456 he was made a Cardinal and he held the titles of Cardinal Bishop of Albano and Porto. Towards 1470 began his relations with Venozza Catanei, the mother of his four children: Juan, Caesar, Lucrezia and Jofre.

Borgia, by a two-thirds majority which was secured by his own vote, became Pope in 1492, and took the name of Alexander VI. He is probably the only Pope who has never found an apologist in spite of the most grievous accusations against him by his contemporaries. Perhaps the kindest thing one can do is to use the words of Leo the Great (440-461) who had declared in his *Third Homily for Christmas Day* that "The dignity of Peter suffers no diminution even in an unworthy successor". Alexander VI died in Rome on the 18th August 1503.

Malachy's prophecy refers to the pope's armorial bearings and his Cardinal titles of Albano and Porto.

DE PARVO HOMINE
From a little man

PIUS III
1503

FRANCESCO TODESCHINI-PICCOLOMINI

Francesco who was a nephew of Pope Pius II, was born in 1439. He had spent his boyhood in destitute circumstances when his uncle took him into his household, bestowed upon him his family name and arms and took charge of his training and education. His uncle appointed him Archbishop of Siena and in 1460 created him Cardinal. After the death of Alexander VI the Cardinals could not agree on a principal candidate and cast their vote in favour of Piccolomini, who though only 64 years old died after a reign of only 26 days, in 1503.

Malachy refers to his family name Piccolomini (parvus homo), in English: little man.

FRUCTUS JOVIS JUVABIT
The fruit of Jupiter will help

JULIUS II
1503 - 1513

GIULIANO DELLA ROVERE

Giuliano della Rovere was born in 1443. He followed his uncle into the Franciscan Order and, after his uncle's elevation to the Papacy as Sixtus IV in 1471, began his public career. In 1471 he was created a Cardinal and held numerous episcopal sees. After the death of Sixtus IV in 1484 Cardinal Rovere played a disreputable role in the election of Innocent VIII. Seeing that his own chances for the Papacy were unfavourable he secured the election of a Pope likely to be a puppet in his hands. After the death of Alexander VI he was again a strong candidate, but he had to allow the sick Piccolomini to become Pope before he was able to secure the Cardinals' votes for himself by bribery and promises. (It was the shortest conclave in the history of the Papacy). Julius II spent money liberally on the erection of magnificent palaces and fortresses. Before he became Pope he was the father of three daughters, one of whom, Felice, he gave in marriage to Giovanni Orsini in 1506. He died in 1513.

The Latin legend (*Fructus Jovis Juvabit*) is a reference to the Pope's armorial bearings. On his arms was an oak tree which was the sacred tree to Jupiter.

DE CRATICULA POLITIANA
From a Politian "gridiron"

L E O X
1513 - 1521

GIOVANNI DE' MEDICI

Giovanni de' Medici was born in 1475 son of Lorenzo de' Medici (the Magnificent) and appointed a Cardinal at the age of thirteen. His educator and mentor was the most distinguished humanist and scholar, Angelo Politiano. In 1494 he had to flee his native city in the habit of a Franciscan monk and made several fruitless attempts to restore the supremacy of his family in Florence. The Medicis returned to favour in 1512 and in 1513 Giovanni, then thirty-seven years old, was elected Pope. During his reign he spent nearly five million ducats and left his successor with a debt of nearly half a million ducats. His creditors faced financial ruin and contemporary publications proclaim "Leo X has consumed three pontificates, the treasure of Julius

II, the revenues of his own reign and those of his successor". He died at Rome in 1521.

"*Craticula*", the "gridiron" refers to his father Laurence the Magnificent and *Politiana* to his mentor. This is by any standard a strange way of describing a person.

LEO FLORENTI(N)US
The lion of Florence

ADRIAN VI
1522 - 1523

ADRIANO FLORENSZ

He is the only Pope of modern times, except Marcellus II, who retained his baptismal name. Born of humble parentage in Utrecht in 1459, his education was sponsored by his mother and also Margaret of Burgundy. In 1506 he became the tutor to the grandson of Emperor Maximillian, the future Charles V. Within the next decade he became Bishop, Grand Inquisitor, Cardinal and finally Regent of Spain. In 1522 the Cardinals elected him unanimously to succeed Pope Leo X. Adrian VI died on the 14th September 1523.

Malachy's legend refers to his family name and to the fact that two lions adorn his arms.

FLOS PILEI ÆGRI
The flower of the ball

CLEMENT VII
1523 - 1534

GIULIO DE' MEDICI

Born in 1478 a few days after the death of his father, Giulio was educated by his uncle Laurence the Magnificent. After his cousin's elevation to the Papacy as Leo X, many honours were bestowed upon him and in 1513 he was made a Cardinal. After Adrian's death Cardinal de' Medici was eventually chosen Pope. He was an Italian Prince, a diplomat first and a spiritual ruler afterwards. He died in 1534.

Flos Pilei Ægri is a reference to the Pope's armorial bearings; on his arms were six torteaux, the top one of which was charged with three fleurs-de-lis. It is during this Pope's reign that the divorce of Katherine of Aragon and Henry VIII's revolt against the Church took place.

HYACINTHUS MEDICORUM
The hyacinth of physicians

PAUL III
1534 - 1549

ALESSANDRO FARNESE

Alessandro was born at Rome in 1468 of an ancient Roman family with a long tradition of service to the Church. His grandfather was commander-in-chief of Papal troops under Eugene IV. Alessandro had an excellent education and with such advantages as birth and talent his advancement in the Church was assured and rapid. In 1493 Alexander VI created him a Cardinal with the title of St Cosmas and Damian. He was a Cardinal for over forty years and finally became Dean of the Sacred College. In 1534 the conclave proclaimed him successor to Clement VII without the formality of a ballot. During his reign a number of religious orders were founded, of which the Jesuits and Ursulines are the best known. He died in 1549.

Earlier interpreters give the Pope's arms as charged with six hyacinths. He was also Cardinal of the title of St Cosmas and Damian, who were both doctors. Malachy's legend appears to refer to these two facts.

DE CORONA MONTANA
Of the mountain crown

JULIUS III
1550 - 1555

Giammaria M. Ciocchi del Monte

Giammaria was born on the 10th September 1487 and studied under the Dominicans. In 1512 he succeeded his uncle Antonio del Monte as Archbishop of Siponto. Under Clement VII he was twice appointed Prefect of Rome and after the sack of the City (1527) was one of the hostages given by Clement VII to the Imperialists. Paul III created him a Cardinal in 1536 and he became the successor to that Pope in 1550 after a conclave of ten weeks. His inactivity during the last three years of his pontificate was caused by frequent and severe attacks of gout. The great blemish in his reign was Nepotism: shortly after his accession he created a youth of seventeen, whom he had picked up in the streets of Palma, a Cardinal. He was also extremely lavish in bestowing ecclesiastical honours and benefices upon his relatives. On the 23rd March 1555 he died in Rome.

Malachy's legend refers to the Pope's armorial bearings: his arms showed laurel crowns and mountains.

FRUMENTUM FLOCCIDUM
(a) Hairy grain
(b) Useless corn

MARCELLUS II
1555

Marcello Cervini

Marcello was born in 1501 and had a spectacular career as Papal secretary, which position offered him great influence in the papal

Curia. Pope Paul III created him a Cardinal in 1539. In 1545 he was appointed one of the three Presidents of the Council of Trent and in 1548 he became Librarian of the Vatican. He was also Bishop of Nicastro and Reggio. After the death of Julius III the thirty-nine Cardinals of the conclave elected Cardinal Cervini to the papacy; however, he died after a reign of only twenty-two days.

Palestrina entitled one of his famous polyphonic masses *Missa Papæ Marcelli* in his honour. The Pope's arms show ears of wheat, while the other reference obviously alludes to the shortness of his pontificate.

DE FIDE PETRI
Of the faith of Peter

PAUL IV
1555 - 1559

GIOVANNI PIETRO CARAFFA

The family into which Giovanni was born in 1476 was one of the most illustrious in Naples and he was introduced to the Papal court in 1494 by his famous uncle Cardinal Oliviero Caraffa. Leo X appointed him Ambassador to England and also retained him as Nuncio in Spain. In 1536 he became Cardinal and later Archbishop of Naples. In 1555 he was elected Pope and Nepotism once again reigned supreme.

EDITOR'S NOTE

Onofrio Panvinio, the historian, died at Palermo on the 7th April, 1568. Pope Paul IV is the last Pope mentioned in his epitome. With his death, the prophecies of St Malachy lose an interpreter of great stature. In his lifetime Panvinio had collected with meticulous thoroughness many details and historical facts about the Popes' lives; he often supplied armorial bearings of the Popes' family and facts which were of the greatest help to other interpreters of Malachy.

During his unfortunate reign occurred the final break between the Church of Rome and England. His pontificate was a great disappointment: he who at the beginning was honoured by a public statue lived to see it thrown down and mutilated by the hostile population of Rome. On the 18th August 1559 he died, and was buried in St Peters, but his body was later transferred to another church.

Paul IV appears to have been better known by his Christian name Pietro; Caraffa is derived from the Latin *cara fides*.

ÆSCULAPII PHARMACUM
(a) The medicine of Æsculapius
(b) The Æsculapius of doctors

PIUS IV
1559 - 1565

GIOVANNI ANGELO DE' MEDICI

This pope was born at Milan in 1499. The Medicis of Milan lived in very humble circumstances and the proud house of Florence of the same name claimed no kindred with them until Cardinal Medici was seated on the Papal throne. After his studies in his twenty eighth year he went to Rome where his talents were appreciated by successive Popes. In the last year of Paul III's reign he was created a Cardinal and Julius III appointed him Commander of the Papal troops. His hostility towards Paul IV worked out to his advantage because the conclave which had assembled to elect that Pope's successor voted for the man who in every respect was Paul's opposite. By acclamation he was pronounced Pope in 1560. He died in 1565.

Malachy's legend appears to be a reference to the Pope's family name, but most interpreters point out that the young Medici had studied medicine and was a qualified doctor.

ANGELUS NEMOROSUS
(a)   The angel of the wood
(b)   The angel of Bosco

PIUS V

1566 - 1572

Antonio Michele Ghisleri

Born of a poor family in 1504 Antonio was educated by the Dominicans and entered that religious order in 1528. Pope Paul IV made him a Bishop in 1556 and a Cardinal in 1557. In the same year he was appointed Inquisitor General for all Christendom. When Pius IV wished to admit a thirteen year old boy into the Sacred College, Cardinal Ghisleri opposed and defeated the Pope and his plans. In 1566 he was elected Pontiff. He died in 1572. During his reign he excommunicated Queen Elizabeth I of England and wrote a letter to Mary Stuart in prison.

The Latin legend refers to the Pope's Christian name Michele (Angelus) and his birthplace (Bosco) Lombardy.

It is important to realise that a number of interpreters of the prophecies were Italians, for some prophecies contain a play upon Italian words. They are unfortunately never explained.

. . . .

GREGORY XIII
1572 - 1585

Ugo Boncompagni

Ugo was born at Bologna in 1502. He studied law and was appointed Judge of the Capitol by Pope Paul III. Paul IV appointed him a Bishop and Pius IV created him a Cardinal in 1564. After the death of Pius V in 1572 he was elected Pope. His main efforts were concentrated on restoring the Catholic faith in those countries that had become Protestant. Historians have severely criticised Gregory XIII for the massacre of the Huguenots on St Bartholomew's day in 1572. No other act of Gregory XIII has gained for him a more lasting fame than his reform of the Julian calendar which was introduced in 1578. He died at Rome in 1585.

Malachy's interpreters give as an explanation for *Medium Corpus Pilarum* the fact that on his shield was a dragon naissant, and that Gregory XIII was created a Cardinal by Pius IV who had six Torteaux (Pilias) on his Coat of Arms.

AXIS IN MEDIETATE SIGNI
An axis in the midst of the sign

SIXTUS V
1585 - 1590

Felice Peretti

Felice was born the son of a gardener in 1521 and it is said of him that as a boy he worked as a swineherd. When nine years old he joined a convent where he was educated and ordained Priest in 1547. He soon became famous as a preacher and Pope Pius IV appointed him Counsellor to the Inquisition at Venice. In 1566 he was created a Bishop by Pius V and in 1570 Cardinal. In 1585 he was elected

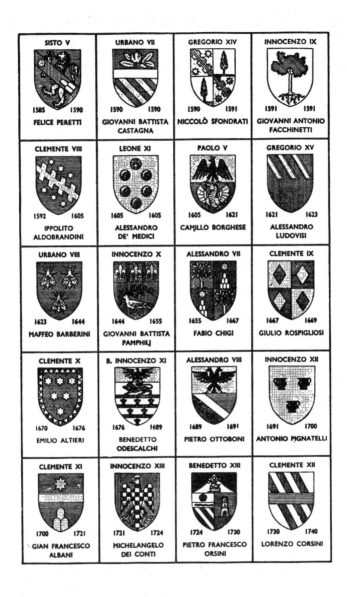

SISTO V	**URBANO VII**	**GREGORIO XIV**	**INNOCENZO IX**
1585 1590	1590 1590	1590 1591	1591 1591
FELICE PERETTI	GIOVANNI BATTISTA CASTAGNA	NICCOLÒ SFONDRATI	GIOVANNI ANTONIO FACCHINETTI
CLEMENTE VIII	**LEONE XI**	**PAOLO V**	**GREGORIO XV**
1592 1605	1605 1605	1605 1621	1621 1623
IPPOLITO ALDOBRANDINI	ALESSANDRO DE' MEDICI	CAMILLO BORGHESE	ALESSANDRO LUDOVISI
URBANO VIII	**INNOCENZO X**	**ALESSANDRO VII**	**CLEMENTE IX**
1623 1644	1644 1655	1655 1667	1667 1669
MAFFEO BARBERINI	GIOVANNI BATTISTA PAMPHILJ	FABIO CHIGI	GIULIO ROSPIGLIOSI
CLEMENTE X	**B. INNOCENZO XI**	**ALESSANDRO VIII**	**INNOCENZO XII**
1670 1676	1676 1689	1689 1691	1691 1700
EMILIO ALTIERI	BENEDETTO ODESCALCHI	PIETRO OTTOBONI	ANTONIO PIGNATELLI
CLEMENTE XI	**INNOCENZO XIII**	**BENEDETTO XIII**	**CLEMENTE XII**
1700 1721	1721 1724	1724 1730	1730 1740
GIAN FRANCESCO ALBANI	MICHELANGELO DEI CONTI	PIETRO FRANCESCO ORSINI	LORENZO CORSINI

Pope after a conclave of four days. After a reign of five years he died in 1590.

Malachy's prophecy is a straightforward allusion to the Pope's coat of arms.

DE RORE CŒLI
From the dew of heaven

URBAN VII
1590

GIOVANNI BATTISTA CASTAGNA

Giovanni Battista was born at Rome in 1521 and was a nephew of Cardinal Jacovazzi. He studied civil and canon law and graduated as a doctor of both. In 1553 he was appointed Archbishop of Rossano and Julius III sent him as Governor to Fano in 1555. In 1573 he resigned his See and Gregory XIII sent him as Nuncio to Venice. In 1583 he was made a Cardinal. Three years later he became Inquisitor General of the Holy Office. He was elected Pope in 1590, on the 15th September, and his reign lasted only 13 days. He died on the 27th September 1590.

Urban VII had been Bishop of Rossano in Calabria where manna called "the dew of heaven" is gathered. (Manna is a sweetish secretion from many trees — as the Manna Ash etc.).

EX ANTIQUITATE URBIS
From the old city

GREGORY XIV
1590 - 1591

NICCOLO' SFONDRATI

Niccolò was born near Milan in 1553. His father Francisco, a Milanese senator, was, after the death of his wife, created a Cardinal by Pope Paul III in 1544. Niccolò was ordained priest and then appointed Bishop of Cremona in 1560. Gregory XIII created him Cardinal Priest of Santa Cecilia in 1583. In 1590 he succeeded Urban VII as Pope. He died in 1591.

De Antiquitate Urbis is another reading of Malachy's legend. It has been suggested that this particular reference in the prophecies was forged during the Conclave by partisans of Cardinal Simoncelli, and was turned into Bishop of Orvieto, in Latin "Urbevetanum — old city"; thus the prophecy was supposed to point out by the above legend that it was the will of providence that this Cardinal be elected Pope. The attempt failed because another Cardinal was elected: Niccolò, from the city of Milan. The explanation was then given that Gregory XIV was a son and grandson of Senators of the city of Milan. Senator comes from the Latin "senex", old man. *De Antiquitate Urbis* could mean "from the ancient of the city". However it could also be said that Milan is an old city having been founded in 400 B.C.

PIA CIVITAS IN BELLO
The pious city at war

INNOCENT IX
1591

GIOVANNI ANTONIO FACCHINETTI

Born in 1519 Giovanni became secretary to a Roman Cardinal and in 1560 Bishop. In 1575 he was appointed Patriarch of Jerusalem and in 1583 created Cardinal of the title of the Four Crowned Martyrs. During the reign of Gregory XIV much of the burden of the Papal administration rested on his shoulders and on the Pontiff's death he was raised to the Papacy. He died in 1591.

Malachy's legend obviously refers to the city of Jerusalem of which the Cardinal was Patriarch before succeeding to the Papacy.

CLEMENT VIII

1592 - 1605

IPPOLITO ALDOBRANDINI

Ippolito was born in 1536. His career was spectacular and he became Cardinal in 1585. His spiritual mentor had been Phillip Neri who remained his confessor for over thirty years. On his elevation to the Papacy Baronius became the Pope's confessor. He died in 1605. The adjective Romulus, meaning Roman, is also mentioned in one of the hymns of the Breviary. The Pope's coat of arms show an embattled bend which is also referred to as a Roman cross. Abbé Cucherat refers to the "cross of Ireland" Clement VIII had to bear at this time because she remained faithful to Rome. There has always been a very special regard for this Pope by the Irish. [During this Pope's reign the twenty-six martyrs of Japan were crucified; their canonisation was reserved for the Pope to whom Malachy had given the description *Crux de Cruce.*]

UNDOSUS VIR

(a) A billowy man
(b) Disappearing like the waves of the sea

LEO XI

1605

ALESSANDRO OTTAVIANO DE' MEDICI

De' Medici was born at Florence in 1535. He became ambassador to Pius V, representing the Duke of Tuscany, which position he held for fifteen years. Gregory XIII made him a Bishop in 1573, Archbishop of Florence in 1574 and Cardinal in 1583. After the death of Clement VIII he was elected Pope, but he died twenty-seven days after his election in 1605.

It has been suggested that Malachy referred to the Pope's short reign. Although not borne out by his Papal coat of arms *"Undosus Vir"* is likely to be an allusion to his heraldic design. A Dutch interpreter of the prophecies of Malachy translates the motto as "A Waterman". There is no explanation concerning Malachy's legend which is completely satisfactory.

GENS PERVERSA
The wicked race

PAUL V
1605 - 1621

CAMILLO BORGHESE

Born in 1550 Camillo's career in the Church was not spectacular. In 1596 he was made a Cardinal by Clement VIII and was appointed Cardinal Vicar of Rome. He was elected Pope in 1605. In 1606 Paul V wrote a letter to James I of England, congratulating him on his succession to the throne, expressing his grief about the plot recently made against the monarch's life and begging the King of England not to make the innocent Catholics suffer for the crime of a few. He promised to exhort all the governors of the realm to be submissive and loyal to their sovereign in all things not opposed to the honour of God. Unfortunately the oath of allegiance demanded by James of his subjects contained clauses which had to be solemnly condemned by the Pope in 1607. This condemnation occasioned the bitter dissension between the monarchy and those governors who submitted to the decision of the Pope. Pope Paul V died in 1621.

The most obvious explanation of Malachy's legend is an allusion to the Pope's armorial bearings which show a dragon and an eagle. These were often referred to as the *Gens Perversa*. There is another interpretation which refers to the war between the Ghibelines and Guelphs whose crests were the dragon and the eagle.

IN TRIBULATIONE PACIS
In the disturbance of peace

GREGORY XV
1621 - 1623

ALESSANDRO LUDOVISI

Alessandro was born in 1554, and became a Judge of the Capitol. In 1612 Paul V appointed him Archbishop of Bologna and it was he who, as Nuncio to Savoy, had to mediate between the Duke of Savoy and King Philip of Spain. In 1616 he was created Cardinal and he was elected successor to Pope Paul V in 1621. The relations between England and the Roman See assumed a more friendly character during his pontificate and Gregory XV was respected by the rulers of the continent, not only in religious affairs but also in matters of a purely political nature. He died in 1623.

Malachy's prophecy is an obvious reference to the Pope's activities as Nuncio which were mainly concerned with the restoration of disturbances which might well have lead to wars.

It is true to say that all the prophecies since Urban VII (1590) are somewhat vague; this has lead critics of the prophecies to suggest that they were indeed forgeries of Cardinal Simoncelli.

LILIUM ET ROSA
The lily and the rose

URBAN VIII
1623 - 1644

Matteo Barberini

He was born in 1568 and educated under the Jesuits. In 1601 he was appointed Papal Legate to France and in 1604 Archbishop of Nazareth. Later he was sent as Nuncio to Paris and in 1606 he was made a Cardinal by Paul V. He was elected Pope in 1623 and throughout his reign he concerned himself with the affairs of France and England. He died in 1644.

There have been many interpretations of Malachy's legend which appear to be a reference to armorial bearings. There is no doubt that his particular interest in the affairs of France (fleur de lis) and England (the rose) seems the most obvious explanation.

JUCUNDITAS CRUCIS
The joy of the cross

INNOCENT X
1644 - 1655

Giovanni Battista Pamphilj

Born in 1574 he became Nuncio at Naples and a Cardinal in 1626. He was elected Pope in 1644. He died in 1655. It is interesting to note that Innocent X was raised to the Pontificate after a long and difficult Conclave on the Feast of the Exaltation of the Cross.

MONTIUM CUSTOS
The guardian of the hills

ALEXANDER VII
1655 - 1667

FABIO CHIGI

Fabio was born in 1599 of one of the most illustrious and powerful Italian families. He entered upon his ecclesiastical career in 1626 and held many posts and responsibilities. In 1651 he became Secretary of State to Innocent X who made him a Cardinal in 1652. In the Conclave of 1655, which lasted eighty days and which is famous for the clash of nation and faction, Chigi was unanimously elected Pope. He died in 1667.

Malachy's legend is an obvious allusion to the Pope's armorial bearings.

SYDUS OLORUM
(a) A star of the swans
(b) The constellation of swans

CLEMENT IX
1667 - 1669

GIULIO ROSPIGLIOSI

Born in 1600 Giulio enjoyed the special favour of Urban VIII who made him Archibishop of Tarsus and sent him as Nuncio to the Spanish Court. In 1657 Alexander VII appointed him Cardinal and ten years later he was elected to the See of St Peter. In 1668 he declared Rose of Lima to be the first American Saint. He died at Rome in December 1669.

The Pope's family came originally from Lombardy where its ancient history is well recorded. The *Teatro Araldico,* a work which gives the armorial bearings of the most ancient and noble families of Italy, describes the Pope's family coat of arms as a shield on which was emblazoned a swan with stars overhead. Another seventeenth century interpretation is that during the conclave this Pope occupied a room which was known as the Chamber of Swans.

DE FLUMINE MAGNO
From the great river

CLEMENT X
1670 - 1676

EMILIO ALTIERI

Emilio was born in 1590, and had a quite unspectacular career in the Church. Clement IX created him Cardinal when he was in his eighties. Unable to secure the election of any of the prominent candidates the Cardinals, after a Conclave of nearly five months, decided on electing a Cardinal of advanced years. Thus Clement X became pontiff. He died in 1676.

Malachy's prophecy concerning this Pope has two possible interpretations: Clement X was born at Rome and in July 1590 the unusual phenomena of the Tiber overflowing its banks is given in Moréri's interpretations of the prophecies. The other explanation is that Malachy's reference is simply a play on words concerning the Pope's name which was Altieri (Alto Reo — a deep river); however, the latter appears to be rather obscure.

BELLUA INSATIABILIS
An insatiable beast

INNOCENT XI
1676 - 1689

BENEDETTO ODESCALCHI

Born in 1611. Benedetto was created a Cardinal by Innnocent X. He was a strong candidate for the Papacy after the death of Clement IX, but the French Government rejected him. After the death of Clement X, King Louis XIV of France again intended to use his real influence against Cardinal Odescalchi's election, but the King yielded to the pressure of the Conclave and after an interregnum of two months he was unanimously elected in 1676 to the Papacy. He died in 1689.

Malachy's legend may be a reference to the Pope's armorial bearings which show a lion and a bird of prey both of which had the reputation of being insatiable beasts. However, contemporary interpreters gave a different explanation of *Bellua Insatiabilis*. It is known that Innocent XI was entirely guided by the views of Cardinal Cibo and this circumstance gave rise to a pun that Innocent XI was "Insatiabilis" for he was never *sine Cibo*, "without Cibo" or "without food".

POENITENTIA GLORIOSA
Glorious repentance

ALEXANDER VIII
1689 - 1691

PIETRO OTTOBONI

Pietro Ottoboni was born in 1610. He enjoyed all the wealth and social position of a descendant of one of the most noble families of Venice. He was made a Cardinal in 1652 and elected to the Papacy in 1689. He died in 1691.

Cucherat thinks that the prophecy refers to the submission and consequent repentance of the Gallican Bishops.

RASTRUM IN PORTA
The rake of the door

INNOCENT XII
1691 - 1700

ANTONIO PIGNATELLI *

Born in 1615 Antonio entered the Roman Curia at the age of twenty. In 1682 he was made a Cardinal and in 1687 Archbishop of Naples. As a compromise the Conclave chose Cardinal Pignatelli to succeed Alexander VIII. He died in 1700.

It is difficult to find a satisfactory explanation for this legend. *Rastrum* means "at hand" or "the next coming on". It could also mean a rake. This word has undergone many changes of meaning in the course of the last five centuries. Such speculation is by no means satisfactory and does not supply a straightforward interpretation of Malachy's prophecy — it is simply guess work.

* Mr. J. L. Todhunter informed me that his "Dictionary of the Popes" gives the name of Innocent XII as Pignatelli del Rastrello. If this name is correct, Malachy's legend would be an obvious reference to the pope's name.

FLORES CIRCUMDATI
Surrounded with flowers

CLEMENT XI
1700 - 1721

GIOVANNI FRANCESCO ALBANI

Giovanni was born in 1649 and at the age of twenty-eight was made a Prelate. In 1690 he was created a Cardinal and the Conclave of 1700 chose him, after deliberating for forty-six days, to be the successor to Innocent XII. He died in 1721.

Urbino, the city where the Pope was born, has a garland of flowers on its coat of arms. It is interesting to note that during the reign of Clement XI a coin was struck and on the exergue were the words "Flores Circumdati". There is no doubt that those who had the medal struck must have been mindful of the prophecies of Malachy which had become not only common property since 1595, but were extremely popular at that time.

DE BONA RELIGIONE
From a good religious background

INNOCENT XIII
1721 - 1724

MICHELANGELO DEI CONTI

He was born in 1655, the son of Carlo II, Duke of Poli. He was created a Cardinal in 1706, and held various offices until in 1721 he was elected Pope in a stormy Conclave. He died in 1724.

This Pope belonged to the famous Conti family which has given so many Popes to the Church. Malachy's legend could therefore be translated "Of a good religious family". This explanation is shared by many medieval interpreters.

MILES IN BELLO
The soldier in battle

BENEDICT XIII
1724 - 1730

PIETRO FRANCESCO ORSINI

Born in 1649, he entered the Dominican order at the age of sixteen against the will of his parents. They appealed in vain to

Clement IX. At the age of twenty-one he was promoted to a professorship and in 1672 elevated to the position of Cardinal. In 1686 a serious illness caused his transfer to Benevento where he remained for thirty-eight years until he was elected Pope in 1724. His first concern as Pope was to enforce rigidly ecclesiastical discipline and he was unsparing in his efforts to abolish luxury and worldly pomp among the Cardinals.

Malachy's legend has always been interpreted to refer to the Pope's constant battle against the pomp and worldly interests of the Curia.

COLUMNA EXCELSA
A lofty pillar

CLEMENT XII
1730 - 1740

LORENZO CORSINI

Lorenzo was born in 1652 and the number of members of his family who had risen to high positions in the Church is innumerable. In 1691 he became Archbishop and Nuncio of Vienna. In 1756 he was created a Cardinal and made Papal Treasurer. His elevation to the Papacy in 1730 caused no surprise. In the second year of his Pontificate he became totally blind. He died in his eighty-eighth year in 1740.

Cucherat interprets the prophecy as an allusion to a bronze statue erected by the Romans to this Pope's memory. The Pope also built a chapel in St John Lateran's where he wished to be buried. Two of the columns in this chapel formerly adorned the portico of the Pantheon of Agrippa. This is another of Cucherat's attempts at explanation.

A reference to Columna is usually an allusion to the fact that one of the Colonna family would succeed to the Papacy.

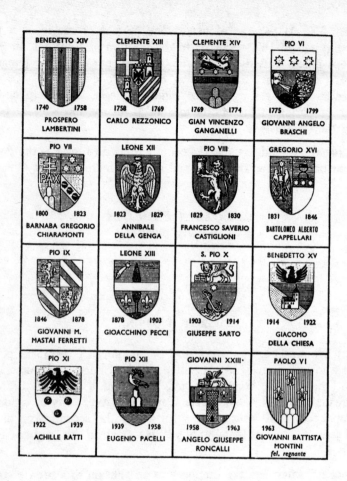

BENEDETTO XIV	CLEMENTE XIII	CLEMENTE XIV	PIO VI
1740 — 1758	1758 — 1769	1769 — 1774	1775 — 1799
PROSPERO LAMBERTINI	CARLO REZZONICO	GIAN VINCENZO GANGANELLI	GIOVANNI ANGELO BRASCHI
PIO VII	LEONE XII	PIO VIII	GREGORIO XVI
1800 — 1823	1823 — 1829	1829 — 1830	1831 — 1846
BARNABA GREGORIO CHIARAMONTI	ANNIBALE DELLA GENGA	FRANCESCO SAVERIO CASTIGLIONI	BARTOLOMEO ALBERTO CAPPELLARI
PIO IX	LEONE XIII	S. PIO X	BENEDETTO XV
1846 — 1878	1878 — 1903	1903 — 1914	1914 — 1922
GIOVANNI M. MASTAI FERRETTI	GIOACCHINO PECCI	GIUSEPPE SARTO	GIACOMO DELLA CHIESA
PIO XI	PIO XII	GIOVANNI XXIII	PAOLO VI
1922 — 1939	1939 — 1958	1958 — 1963	1963
ACHILLE RATTI	EUGENIO PACELLI	ANGELO GIUSEPPE RONCALLI	GIOVANNI BATTISTA MONTINI fel. regnante

ANIMAL RURALE
Animal of the field

BENEDICT XIV
1740 - 1758

Prospero Lorenzo Lambertini

Prospero was born in 1675 and at the age of nineteen he received the degrees of Doctor of Theology and Doctor of Canon and Civil Law. In 1727 he was made Bishop and in 1728 Cardinal. When Clement XII died the Conclave lasted for six months and the election then seemed no nearer than at the beginning. Cardinal Lambertini, who had been proposed as a compromise, addressed the Conclave saying: "If you wish to elect a saint, choose Gotti; a statesman, Aldabrandini; an honest man, elect me". Lambertini was chosen and took the name of Benedict XIV. He died in 1758.

There appears to be no reason for interpreting the legend as an allusion to the Pope's armorial bearings. Interpreters stress the fact that the Pope wrote away at his desk like a "plodding ox", which, according to the old writers, was typical of the persevering steady worker. (St Thomas Aquinas was called the dumb ox by his fellow students because he fed his mind and ruminated silently.)

ROSA UMBRIÆ
The rose of Umbria

CLEMENT XIII
1758 - 1769

Carlo Rezzonico

Carlo was born at Venice in 1693 and became Bishop of Padua in 1743. In 1747 he became a Cardinal and in 1758 he was elected Pope. He died in 1769.

The interpretations given to Malachy's legend appear somewhat far fetched; however, during his Pontificate he raised to the dignity of saints a great number of persons belonging to the Franciscan order, mystically called *Rosa Umbriæ*.

URSUS VELOX
The swift bear

CLEMENT XIV

1769 - 1774

LORENZO (or Giovanni Vincenzo Antonio) GANGANELLI

He was born in 1705. He received his education from the Jesuits of Rimini and at the age of nineteen he entered the order of the Franciscans. Clement XIII gave him the Cardinal's hat in 1759 and the Conclave of 1769 chose him to succeed Clement XIII. Under his pontificate the Jesuits were suppressed. He died in 1774.

Without producing any evidence, the American interpreter Robb states that the Pope's family coat of arms showed a running bear. However, with the death of Panvinio we lose much of the information which helped earlier interpreters.

Wion, O'Kelly and Cucherat try in vain to give a reasonable explanation of this legend. There is no bear in the arms of the Pope and to my mind it is unlikely that the imminent French revolution is typified in Malachy's description. This is again one of the instances where any interpretation would be purely guess work.

PEREGRINUS APOSTOLICUS
The pilgrim pope
PIUS VI
1775 - 1799

GIOVANNI ANGELICO BRASCHI

Giovanni was born in 1717. He became Papal secretary in 1755 and Clement XIV made him a Cardinal in 1755. After this, he retired to the Abbey of Subiaco (of which he was Abbot) until his election in the same year. He died in 1799.

The legend is usually explained by the well known facts of the Pope's life. His extremely long Pontifical reign had led contemporary writers to refer to him as the Apostolic Pilgrim on Earth.

AQUILA RAPAX
A rapacious eagle

PIUS VII
1800 - 1823

BARNABA CHIARAMONTI

This pope was born in 1740 and his elevation to the Papacy was foretold, as Pius VII himself later related, by his mother, who in 1763 had entered the convent of Carmelites. Pius VI created him a Cardinal in 1786 and the Conclave elected him Pope in 1800. He died in 1823.

The Pope's pontificate was overshadowed by Napoleon whose emblem was the eagle.

CANIS ET COLUBER
A dog and a serpent

LEO XII
1823 - 1829

ANNIBALE DELLA GENGA

Born in 1760, Annibale became a Priest at the age of only twenty-three. In 1820 he was made Vicar of Rome and after Pius VII's death was elected to the Papacy. He died in 1829.

I think it is fair to say that if the order of two successive Popes could be reversed, the allusion to armorial bearings would fit perfectly. What better description for Leo XII than that which was given to Pius VII *"Aquila Rapax"* and how perfectly would Pius VII have been described with the legend *"Custus Montium"* or *"Crux de Cruce"*, if chance would have had it so.

Contrary to popular belief, the original manuscript of the Prophecies of Malachy has not been found in the Vatican Library. His Excellency Archbishop Cardinale instigated a thorough search for the manuscript at the Vatican. The sad fact is that there is no *record* of this manuscript being there or having been there. The many publications and additions to Malachy's prophecies since the middle of the sixteenth century do not concur exactly with the order of the Popes, particularly during the reigns of the antipopes. It is also reasonable to assume that the interpreters have relied largely on the works of their predecessors, adopting the same order of succession.

As matters stand Malachy's prophecy concerning Leo XII may be a reference to two of the Pope's most outstanding virtues: vigilance, which one associates with a dog; and prudence, commonly associated with the serpent.

VIR RELIGIOSUS
A religious man

PIUS VIII
1829 - 1830

Francesco Saverio Castiglioni

Francesco was born in 1761 and attended a Jesuit school. In 1800 Pius VII appointed him Bishop of Moltalto and he held various episcopal sees. As early as the Conclave of 1823 Castiglioni was among the candidates for the Papacy. Cardinal Wiseman relates that this Pope's elevation to the Papacy, as well as the name he was to assume, was predicted by Pius VII for, on a certain occasion, the Pope addressed Cardinal Castiglioni and said, "Your Holiness Pius VIII may one day settle this matter". At the election of 1829 he succeeded Leo XII and he died on the 1st December 1830.

Malchy's legend may refer to the fact (Religiosus) that the Pope had come from a family which was well known for its deep faith and that he was not the first Pope this family had given to the Church. Other interpreters have taken *Religiosus* to mean the same as Pius, thus foreshadowing his name.

DE BALNEIS ETRURIÆ
From the baths of Etruria

GREGORY XVI
1831 - 1846

Mauro, or Bartolomeo Alberto Cappellari

Mauro was born in 1765 and upon entering the Camaldolese Monastery of San Michele di Murano took the name Mauro. Three years later he was professed and ordained priest in 1787. In 1800

Dom Mauro became Abbot. In 1825 Leo XII created him Cardinal and Prefect of the Congregation and Propaganda. Following the death of Pope Pius VIII he was elected to the See of St Peter in 1831. He died in 1846.

Gregory XVI started his religious life in the order of Camaldolese which was founded in the thirteenth century in a locality called in Latin *Balneum*, in Etruria. Under the Pope's personal supervision the most exquisite discoveries were made during the Etruscan excavations. The museum which contains these discoveries of ancient Etruscan art was in fact called after his name the "Gregorian Museum". The Pope's armorial bearings show on the dexter side the arms of the Camaldolese.

CRUX DE CRUCE
The cross from a cross

PIUS IX
1846 - 1878

GIOVANNI MARIA MASTAI FERRETTI

Giovanni Maria was born in 1792 and was admitted to the Pope's noble court in 1814. He was refused admission to the priesthood on the grounds that he suffered from epilepsy and proceeded to study theology at the Roman Seminary. His health was completely restored by 1819 when he was ordained Priest. By 1827 he was created Archbishop and in 1840 he was made a Cardinal. In 1846, two weeks after the death of Gregory XVI, Cardinal Mastai Ferretti was elected Pope.

The loss of his temporal power was only one of the many trials that filled the long pontificate of Pius IX. There was scarcely a country where the rights of the Church were not infringed upon. In many countries church property was confiscated, religious orders were expelled and Bishops imprisoned or banished. The height of these disturbances was reached during the Kulturkampf inaugurated in 1873. Pius IX is well remembered for ordaining to important ecclesiastical positions only such men as were famous for both piety and learning. Among the great Cardinals created by him were Wiseman and Manning for England, Cullen for Ireland and McCloskey for the United States. On the 29th September 1850 he re-established the Catholic hierarchy in England by erecting the Archdiocese of Westminster with twelve Suffragan Sees. He died in Rome on the 7th February 1878.

Although a reference to the cross reoccurs frequently in the prophecies, there is little doubt that Pius IX had to bear the heaviest cross yet to be inflicted upon the Papacy. The temporal powers of the Church had been drastically curtailed and the influence of the spiritual leader of the Catholic world reduced. There is no doubt that the House of Savoy, whose emblem is a cross, added greatly to the afflictions of this Pope.

LUMEN IN CŒLO
A light in the sky

LEO XIII
1878 - 1903

GIOACCHINO PECCI

Gioacchino was born in 1810 and became a Priest in 1837. In 1843 he was appointed a Nuncio and consecrated Archbishop. In 1853 Pius IX made him a Cardinal. The Conclave of 1878 elected him Pope.

Among the instances of Leo XIII's influence in the English speaking world may be mentioned the elevation of John Henry Newman to the Cardinalate, the beatification of forty English martyrs, two Encyclicals *Ad Anglos* of 1895 on the return to Catholic unity, and

Apostolicæ Curæ of 1896 on the non validity of Anglican Orders. In Ireland he created Archbishop McCabe a Cardinal and in the United States he founded the Apostolic Delegation in Washington in 1892. Leo XIII died on the 20th July 1903.

This is the first of Malachy's legends since 1590 which appears to be a straightforward allusion to the Pope's armorial bearings which shows a blazing star in his coat of arms. The same blazing comet has occurred already in the arms of Innocent VII and the prophet refers to it as *"sydus"*. It has often been suggested that if Malachy's legend concerning Leo XIII read *"sydus in cœlo"* it would be more convincing. However, the fact remains that *"Lumen in Cœlo"* is a fairly good description of the Papal coat of arms.

IGNIS ARDENS
The burning fire

PIUS X

1903 - 1914

GIUSEPPE SARTO

Giuseppe was born in 1835 and was ordained in 1858. In 1884 he was appointed Bishop of Mantua and in 1893 he became Patriarch of Venice and a Cardinal. He was probably the most zealous propagandist of his time. Before all else, his efforts were directed to the promotion of piety among the faithful. After the death of Leo XIII Cardinal Sarto was elected Pope. He died in 1914.

Without wishing to over-stress the point, *"Ignis Ardens"* most aptly describes this Pope, whose zeal and endeavour were directed towards the spiritual renaissance of the Church he headed.

RELIGIO DEPOPULATA
Religion laid waste

BENEDICT XV
1914 - 1922

GIACOMO DELLA CHIESA

Born in 1854 he spent most of his life in the diplomatic service. In 1907 he became Archbishop of Bologna and in 1914 Cardinal and Pope. During the First World War the Pope made many attempts to bring about peace and to relieve suffering. He died in 1922.

The years of Pope Benedict's reign were overshadowed by the death of millions of Christians in World War I. 1917 saw the beginning of the Russian revolution which brought about the end of religious life in this formerly most Christian country.

Religio Depopulata is one of Malachy's prophecies which have unfortunately been fulfilled true to the letter of the word.

FIDES INTREPIDA
Unshaken faith

PIUS XI
1922 - 1939

ACHILLE RATTI

Achille Ratti was born in 1857. He was appointed Prefect of the Vatican Library in 1914, Papal Nuncio to Poland in 1919 and Cardinal Archbishop of Milan in 1921. Elevated to the Papacy in 1922 he faced the rise of Fascism and Communism in the Western world. He died in 1939.

Recent publications of Vatican documents show the tremendous pressure which was put on this Pope by the dictators of Italy and Germany. Again one could say that it was the Pope's *"Fides Intrepida'* — his unshaken faith — in what he believed to be right which may have prevented even greater hardship than that which befell the Catholic Church during his reign. His courage at which Hitler sneered and raged and before which Mussolini crumbled; his outspoken criticism against Fascism and Communism which upset the ruthless plans of the dictators, and his unshaken faith, all sustained the Church in a period of the most severe trials. Malachy's description appears to be a most fitting one for Pope Pius XI.

PASTOR ANGELICUS
An angelic shepherd

PIUS XII
1939 - 1958

EUGENIO PACELLI

Born in 1876 Eugenio Pacelli spent most of his career in the diplomatic service. From 1917 until 1929 he was Nuncio in Germany and in 1930 he became Cardinal Secretary of State. His elevation to the Papacy in 1939 was a matter of formality because no other person could have followed in the steps of his predecessor more aptly. Pius XII died in 1958.

Recent publications, particularly that by Pinchas Lapide (*The Last Three Popes and the Jews*, Souvenir Press, 1967) and the publication of the Vatican documents relating to the reign of Pius XII, have given to the world unshakable and irrefutable proof of this Pope's greatness and spirituality. He was in the truest sense of the word an Angelic Pastor to the flock committed to his care, and his flock were all those who suffered. In spite of the defamatory and scurrilous allegations published about him in such contemporary plays as *The Representative* by Rolf Hochhuth, Pius XII has emerged as one of the great Popes of all time. Although the contents of his visions have not yet become public knowledge there is little doubt that his affinity to the spiritual world was a very real and close one. The description *Pastor Angelicus* is most apt and one of the most descriptive ones in Malachy's prophecies.

PASTOR ET NAUTA
Pastor and mariner

JOHN XXIII
1958 - 1963

ANGELO GIUSEPPE RONCALLI

Born in 1881 Giuseppe Roncalli spent many years as Apostolic Delegate and Nuncio in Turkey, Greece, Bulgaria and France. In 1953 he was created a Cardinal and appointed Patriarch of Venice and in 1958 the Conclave elected him Pope. In 1962 he convened the second Vatican Council and his Encyclical *Pacem in Terris* (1963) is considered one of the greatest documents of our time. He died in 1963.

Pope John was the pastor of the world and perhaps more loved by Catholics and non-Catholics alike than any other Pope in history. Malachy's legend *Pastor et Nauta** points immediately to the See of Venice which indeed he occupied as Patriarch before his elevation to the Papacy.

During the conclave the rumour circulated in Rome that Cardinal Spellman of New York, who was known to be very interested in the Prophecies of Malachy, had hired a boat, filled it with sheep and sailed up and down the river Tiber.

FLOS FLORUM
(Flower of Flowers)

PAUL VI

GIOVANNI BATTISTA MONTINI

1963 - 1978

Born in 1897 he worked with his predecessors in the papal Secretariat of State and became Sostituto (Pro-Secretary of State). In 1958 he became Archbishop of Milan and was made a Cardinal. The Conclave elected him Pope in 1963.

Once again the armorial bearings appear to have given an interpretation. In his shield were three fleurs-de-lis. Some interpreters believe that the Pope was strongly influenced by French advisers and that the Latin description *Flos Florum* applied as much to their influence as to the papal arms.

THE YEAR OF THE THREE POPES

The events of 1978 have caused great concern among the students of St. Malachy's prophecies. The death of Pope Paul VI brought about much speculation. There were many Cardinals who found themselves hailed as *papabile*, likely candidates for the forthcoming election. There were even some eminent prelates who knew that they were *papabile*, and a few who actually thought that they were Pope and the election merely a formality.

The Prophecies of Malachy were much quoted but rarely interpreted, and although Cardinal Giovanni Benelli, like Pope Paul VI a former Sostituto, and now Cardinal Archbishop of Florence, was a favourite among punters, none of the newspapers picked up the Malachy interpretation much favoured inside the Vatican — a wrong but plausible one — that Florence was situated in the centre of the former diocese of Luna. As it turned out, Cardinal Benelli was not elected.

DE MEDIETATE LUNAE
(Of the half moon)

JOHN PAUL I

ALBINO LUCIANI

1978

In my interpretation in the first edition of the Prophecies which I edited in 1968, ten years before the prophecy was to be fulfilled, I suggested that this could be an allusion to some great event concerning those whose religious life is lived under the sign of the half moon. I continued: "The speculations in which one could engage here are numerous, particularly at a time when the Middle East situation could prove the most dangerous threat to peace in our time. Such a conflict might well lead to a 'Holy War' which would be fought under the half moon and would have devastating effects and repercussions on Muslims and Christians alike."

On August 26, 1978 the Conclave elected Albino Luciani the Cardinal Patriarch of Venice, Pope. He assumed the name John Paul I. Those who had expected that the new Pope might have armorial bearings showing a half moon were disappointed. In fact his papal coat of arms was designed by Archbishop Heim, who had previously drawn up the arms for Popes John XXIII and Paul VI, and in accordance with the Pope's wishes these arms were composed from charges in the shields of the two predecessors whose names he had adopted.

The totally unexpected death of the Pope thirty three days later stunned the world. So great was the shock that few — if any — of those who had engaged in endless speculations before the Pope's election had realised that certain political events then taking place in the United States of America, seemed to bear out my interpretation of ten years ago. The President of Egypt and the Prime Minister of Israel were guests of the American President at Camp David and had started peace talks. Unfortunately, the dates set for a ratification of those peace negotiations passed by without the peace treaty having been signed, and subsequent developments have now shown that even if such a treaty between Israel and Egypt were to materialise, it would probably cause an uprising among other Muslim nations and lead to that dreaded 'Holy War'. The thirty three days of the Pope's reign were eventful days, and the half moon which then rose on the horizon may well over-shadow many decades to come. And while Camp David dominated world affairs, the Half Moon began rising in Paris, where the exiled Ayatollah Khomeini incited his followers to a "Holy War". On the anniversary of the day when Pope John Paul I was elected to the See of St Peter the Islamic revolution already counted its victims by the thousands.

It seems surprising that St. Malachy made no real references to the very short reign of some popes. Although Pope John Paul's short reign has been called unique by many commentators, there have been twelve popes who had an even shorter reign, and five of them since the Prophecies of Malachy were written. Celestine IV reigned seventeen days in 1241, Pius III twenty six days in 1503, Marcellus II twenty two days in 1555, Urban VII thirteen days in 1590 and Leo XI twenty seven days in 1605.

Only twice have interpreters of Malachy managed to find a possible, though unlikely, translation of the Latin prophecy which could have referred to the short reign. In both cases it is an alternative translation of a Latin phrase and not one the late Archbishop of Armagh is likely to have had in mind. "FRUMENTUM FLOCCIDUM" which applied to Pope Marcellus II, could be translated "useless corn", and with some imagination be an allusion to a short reign. Even more far fetched is the alternative translation for "UNDOSUS VIR" as "dis-appearing like the waters of the sea", which referred to Pope Leo XI.

The shortest reign was that of Pope Stephen II in 752 AD (who was only a priest when elected) and who died after only three days, before he was even consecrated bishop.

DE LABORE SOLIS
From the toil of the sun
Of the eclipse of the sun

JOHN PAUL II

KAROL WOJTYLA

1978 -

If the *SEDE VACANTE* period following the death of Pope Paul VI were to be described as 'buzzing with rumours' and a 'time for ambitious prelates to play the field', the weeks leading up to the election of the next pope were not very edifying to those who still believed that the Holy Ghost would descend upon a chosen one. It seemed as if the Holy Ghost had been banned from Rome. One could be forgiven for comparing those days with papal election fever of centuries past, when secular power politics played an important role.

I believe we witnessed the greatest miracle of this century when Cardinal Karol Wojtyla of Poland was elected Pope in November 1978. If ever the power of the Holy Spirit has been seen to work quickly and effectively, it was when this holy man stepped onto the balcony to show himself to his people as the 263rd Pastor of the Universal Church.

The Holy Spirit appears to have made his choice with total disregard for the Prophecies of St. Malachy and certainly with contempt for the possible interpretation I gave in 1968. On the other hand the Holy Spirit was not influenced by the politicians inside the conclave either. I had considered two possible interpretations: one which would allude to the Pope's coat of arms, and one alluding to an eclipse of the sun on certain dates.

The coat of arms of Pope Paul II makes no allusion to a burning sun, and as for the many permutations of eclipses of the sun I had worked out, none of them applied.

Considering the evolution of the papacy since the death of Paul VI and the deep interest John Paul II takes, not just in Africa and South America, but in the entire third world, De Labore Solis is an obvious reference to those continents and countries that toil under the burning sun - the Arab World and all those countries roughly lying between the Tropics of Cancer and Capricorn. Had there existed a concept of a third world in his time, I am confident Malachy would have used that phrase for the fastest growing part of the Catholic Church that has dominated the pontificate of John Paul II as much as he has dominated it. The legacy John Paul II inherited from his predecessor, John Paul I, does not bode well for the Church and for him personally. The growth of Islamic fundamentalism, its fanatical fight against so-called Western ideas and influences, the Church and especially the papacy has not as yet reached its zenith, whatever the moderates of the Arab and Western worlds may hope. John Paul II has the personal strength to eclipse 'De medietate Lunae', but as past prophecies have shown when events rather than personalities were prophecied, future popes appear still to be subject to their influences.

GLORIAE OLIVAE
The glory of the olive

The glory of the olive could occupy the See of St. Peter whilst the olive branch of peace and harmony is broken, or he could be the ultimate peacemaker; perhaps the the next Pope holds out the olive branch to the wrong people only to show the waiting faithful some useless piece of paper with "peace in our time" written on it.

The olive branch has always been associated with peace and this description might have been most fittingly applied to Pope Pius XII as a reference to his coat of arms. There is little doubt that this legend can be more easily explained in the future than the one before.

Some early interpreters have gone out of their way to stress that Malachy in his prophecies does not specifically state that no Popes shall reign between *Gloriae Olivae* and the last, *Petrus Romanus*; nor on the other hand does he mention that there will be others.

The Order of St Benedict has claimed by tradition that this pope will come from within the Order. St Benedict himself has prophecied that before the end of the world comes about, his Order will triumphantly lead the Catholic Church in its fight against evil. The Benedictines are also known as the Olivetans, which may well account for another interpretation of the prophecy. With the election of Benedictine monks to the College of Cardinals, this interpretation appears a very favoured one.

PETRUS ROMANUS

The final legend is self-explanatory as Malachy concludes by stating that:-

"In the final persecution of the Holy Roman Church there will reign Peter the Roman, who will feed his flock among many tribulations; after which the seven-hilled city will be destroyed and the dreadful Judge will judge the people."

AUTHOR'S NOTE ON THE
FOURTH EDITION

Apart from numerous reprints since 1969, this is the fourth revised edition. What started ten years ago as a favour to my friend, Harold Clarke, M.A., of Dublin, namely editing the prophecies for a limited publication of 1,500 copies, has snowballed into one of the most popular and widely published books I have been associated with.

Several foreign language editions have appeared and in the U.S.A. two publishers brought out a hardback and paperback edition. I have been somewhat bewildered and worried when I read the additional forewords and prefaces that appeared in those editions. In it, the writers credit me with all possible gifts. Casually listening to my car radio not so long ago, the prophecies of Malachy were the subject of a discussion on betting! Apparently my book was being used by punters as a form book for placing bets on future popes. Cardinal Angelo Dell'Acqua, who unfortunately died shortly after I heard the programme on the B.B.C., was the firm favourite for *De Medietate Lunae*; which only goes to show how foolish it is to indulge in such fancies.

August 1979   Peter Bander

FOREWORD

THE ARCHBISHOP OF ARMAGH, HIS GRACE THE MOST REV. DR. G. O. SIMMS, has asked me to write a brief foreword to these prophecies since I was the first Protestant clergyman to open the Oireachtas (which roughly answers to the Eisteddfod) and have a certain nodding acquaintance with these matters.

It is doubtful whether we have anything from the hand of Saint Columbkille but a rather dull latin hymn, *Altus Prosator*. Our Church of Ireland Hymn Book contains a version of an Irish hymn ascribed to him translated by McGregor as *Alone with none but thee my God*. Indeed, there are many such compositions, including his *Farewell to Ireland*, some of them exquisitely beautiful. But they are in Middle Irish, there is nothing attributed to him in really old Irish. The same may be said of the original Irish version of these prophecies, which indeed have been modernised to some extent.

E. A. Anderson wrote in the *Zeitschrift fur Keltische Philologie* "The peculiar characteristic of a prophetic history, and probably the reason for its composition, was that it could be carried beyond the time at which it was recited, either with a view to obtaining the favour of a reigning king, or with a view to influencing the course of events."

It is a pity that this is only a reprint of the prophecies. A Critical Edition embodying some philological and historical research might be of considerable interest and might even throw some light on past history, in these days when it is at last possible to write accurate history and when we have given up bitter controversy for friendly dialogue and can see how much we have in common with our fellow men and fellow Christians and fellow Irishmen.

W. COSLETT QUIN
Canon of the Prebendal Stall of Swords,
St Patrick's Cathedral, Dublin.

The
Prophecies
of
St. Columbkille

Abbot of Iona
concerning the people
& country of
Ireland
with an introduction
by
Peter Bander
and notes
written in 1855
by
Nicholas O'Kearney

INTRODUCTION

To say that the Prophecies of St. Columbkille are controversial is just a typical English understatement. There are those who for political reasons want them to be authentic and genuine; others are equally determined to dismiss them as outright forgeries. In his foreword, Canon Coslett Quin strikes a very cautious note, expressing his regret that this is a reprint of the prophecies which have been circulating for some centuries and not a proper philological study of Columbkille's actual work. Reading between the lines, it is obvious that Canon Quin does not accept them as genuine or authentic writings of the Irish Saint.

Naturally, the question arises why publish them and perpetuate the myth of the prophecies? The fact remains that they have become an integral part of Irish life and folklore. To many Irishmen they are the foundation upon which they build their dreams for the future. Because Columbkille and Malachy make up the substantial part of the prophetic pre-occupation of the Irish, I was asked to incorporate them both in one volume. In 1855, Nicholas O'Kearney published for the first time his notes on Columbkille's prophecies; although during the last two centuries, a number of different versions of the prophecies have been circulating, there have always been two main forms which, for better or worse, alternated in being presented as the only authentic record of Columbkille's visions: the one reproduced here, which O'Kearney claims originates from the hand of the Saint himself, and another written by Adomnan, Abbot of Iona from 679 until his death in 704.

The only way of checking on the authenticity would be to go to St. Patrick's College in Maynooth where, so it has been stated for centuries, "the original Irish version is available for the perusal of the student, thus enabling him to check the translation and study the original language in order to ensure antiquity" (to quote from a recent introduction to the prophecies by Professor Tom Marriott in Australia). The point is that the archivist at Maynooth, indeed one of the most respected and comprehensive sources of information for scholars, will tell you that there is no record of any prophecies of Columbkille ever having been in the possession of the College; nor does he know of any place where they possibly could be. Yet, study any of the previous publications, and you will find that Maynooth, with all the authority this learned place carries, is given as the trustees of Columbkille's original manuscript.

The other version of the prophecies is contained in Adomnan's *Life of Columbkille*. His biography of the founder of the Abbey of Iona has been described as "the most complete piece of biography that all Europe can boast of, not only at so early a period but even through the whole Middle Ages." Written nearly a hundred years after Columbkille's death, Adomnan compiled a record of traditions of the Saint's life from oral and written sources. The oral authorities, Adomnan assured his readers, were chosen from among a great many for their reliability so far as that could be ascertained.

The life of Columbkille (Columba), Abbot of Iona, is well documented. He was born at Gartan, County Donegal in Ireland on 7 December 521; he belonged to the Clan O'Donnell and was of royal descent. He entered the monastic school of Moville under St. Finnian and became a deacon. Later he entered the monastery of Clonard where he became one of those twelve Clonard disciples known in subsequent history as "The Twelve Apostles of Ireland". After a pestilence which devastated Ireland in 544, Columbkille returned to Ulster and the following years were marked by the founding of many important monasteries. At the age of forty-four he left Ireland and landed at Iona on 12 May 563. The thirty-two remaining years of his life were mainly spent in preaching the Christian faith to the inhabitants of the glens and wooded straths of Northern Scotland. However, he frequently visited Ireland. From Iona he governed those numerous communities in Ireland and Scotland which regarded him as their father and founder. This accounts for the unique position occupied by his successors as Abbot of Iona, who governed those provinces, although they had received priests' orders only. It was considered unbecoming that any successor in the office of Abbot of Iona should possess a dignity higher than that of the founder. Bishops were regarded as being of a superior order, but subject nevertheless to the jurisdiction of the Abbot.

Columbkille is said never to have spent an hour without study, prayer, writing or similar occupations. During his lifetime he is said to have written some three hundred books, two of which, *The Book of Durrow* and the psalter called *The Cathach* have been preserved. He died on 9 June 597. For purposes of controversy it has been maintained that Columbkille ignored papal supremacy, because he entered on his mission without the Pope's authorisation. Adomnan is silent on the subject. However, in those days a mandate from the Pope was not deemed to be essential for the work which Columbkille undertook. The Stowe Missal which represents the Mass of the Celtic Church during the early part of the seventh century, contains in its Canons prayers for the Pope more enthusiastic and emphatic than those of the Roman Liturgy. Another point which has been held against Columbkille is the complete absence of the "cultus of Our Lady".

There is little doubt that Columbkille was a prolific writer; moreover he was actively engaged in political warfare and influential in shaping the destiny of his countrymen. It is reasonable to assume that he wrote down something like prophecies, though they were based on his wide knowledge of political events around him. Ambiguity is the hallmark of any good political writer; without committing himself to foretelling specific events, the general trend of future happenings can easily be outlined in broad terms. What makes the Prophecies of Columbkille so topical is the simple fact that history repeats itself, especially Irish history. No country has suffered for so long and so cruelly under centuries of oppression as Ireland has. It is therefore not surprising that the simple and pious people turn to their long dead Saints for comfort and hope. The prophecies of Columbkille are just another straw to cling on to; after all, which Irishman would not subscribe whole-heartedly to the last verse of "The Independent Man", which concludes the Prophecies of Columbkille:

> The new Eire shall be Eire the prosperous,
> Great shall be her renown and her power,
> There shall not be on the surface of the wide earth,
> A country found to equal this fine country!

PROPHECIES OF ST. COLUMBKILLE

ADDRESSED TO ST. BRENDAN

The time shall come O Brendan[1],
When you would feel it painful to reside in Erin;
The sons of kings shall be few in number,
And the *literati* shall be deprived of dignity.

They (the people) will continue to reside in stone mansions,
They will inhabit the islets on the lakes;
They will not perform charitable acts,
And truth shall not remain in them.

They will plunder the property of the church,
They will take preys of cattle furtively;
They will treat men of learning disrespectfully,
Afterwards they themselves shall become powerless.

The sons of kings (great men) will become archæologists,
The descendants of sages shall become ignorant;
They will be continually sneering at each other,
They will employ themselves at reading and writing.

They will scoff at acts of humanity,
And at irreproachable humility;
Men of learning shall become rare among them,
And ignorant men shall prosper.

---

[1] *O'Brendain.* This was St. Brendan whom St. Columbkille is represented as addressing; probably, the poem was a letter from St. Columbkille to his friend.

There shall come times of dark affliction,
Of scarcity, of sorrow, and of wailing;
In the latter ages of the world's existence,
And monarchs will be addicted to falsehood.

Neither justice nor covenant will be observed,
By any one people of the race of Adam;
They will become hard-hearted and penurious,
And will be devoid of piety.

Men will become murmurers,—
The trees shall not bear the usual quantity of fruit;
Fisheries shall become unproductive,
And the earth shall not yield its usual abundance.

The clergy will become fosterers,
In consequence of the tidings of wretchedness, (that will reach them);
Churches shall be held in bondage, (i.e. become private property),
By the all-powerful men of the day.

Inclement weather, and famine shall come,
Hatred, malignity, and despair;
The natural span of human life shall be abridged,
And fishes will forsake the rivers.

The people oppressed by want of food, shall pine to death,
Meanwhile they shall be bound in slavery;
And in consequence of their enmity to one another,
Dreadful storms and hurricanes shall afflict them.

Judges will administer injustice,
Under the sanction of powerful, outrageous kings;
The common people will adopt false principles,
Oh, how lamentable shall be their position!

Doctors of science shall have cause to murmur,
They will become niggardly in spirit;
The aged will mourn in deep sorrow,
On account of the woeful times that shall prevail.

Cemeteries shall become all red (dug up),
In consequence of the wrath that will follow sinners;
Wars and contentions shall rage,
In the bosom of every family.

Kings (great men) shall be steeped in poverty,
They will become inhospitable to their guests;
The voice of the parasite will be more agreeable to them
Than the melody of the harp touched by the sages' finger.

Their candles shall be quenched,
Without intermission each sabbath day;
In consequence of the general prevalence of sinful practices,
Humility shall produce no fruit.

The professors of science shall not be rewarded,
Amiability shall not characterize the people;
Prosperity and hospitality shall not exist,
But niggardliness and destitution will assume their place.

The changes of seasons shall produce only half their verdure,
The regular festivals of the church will not be observed;
All classes of men shall be filled,
With hatred and enmity towards each other.

The people will not associate affectionately with each other,
During the great festivals of the seasons;
They will live devoid of justice and rectitude,
Up from the youth of tender age to the aged.

The clergy shall be led into error,
By the misinterpretation of their reading;
The relics of the saints will be considered powerless,
Every race of mankind will become wicked!

They will construct islands,
Upon the pools of clear water (lakes);
Numberless diseases shall then prevail,
When Ath-na-cuilte[2] shall be drained.

Sons of kings will not have sureties of kine.
Fortifications will be built narrow;
During those times of dreadful danger,
Persons born to inheritances shall be sorrowful.

Young women will become unblushing,
And aged people will be of irascible temper;
The kine will seldom be productive, as of old;
Lords will become murderers.

Young people will decline in vigour,
They will despise those who shall have hoary hair;
There shall be no standard by which morals may be regulated,
And marriages will be solemnized without witnesses.

Troublous shall be the latter ages of the world,
According to the Book of Truth :—
The clergy shall become ignorant,
Concerning the real festivities of the church.

The dispositions of the generality of men I will point out,
From the time they shall abandon hospitable habits—
With the view of winning honour for themselves,
They will hold each other as objects for ridicule.

I am Columbkille,
A prophet that speaks with perspicuity;
I can discern in my little book,
The clear explanation of all knowledge.

The possessors of abundance shall fall,
Through the multiplicity of their falsehoods;
Covetousness shall take possession of every glutton,
And when satiated their arrogance will know no bounds.

---

2 *Ath-na-cuilte*. In one copy *Ath-na-helite*. Most commentators suppose this place to be the present Annahilt, near Hillsborough, county of Down, contiguous to which is now a bog, probably the state of drainage to which reference is made in the text.

Between the mother and daughter,
Anger and bitter sarcasms shall continuously exist;
Neighbours will become treacherous,
Cold, and false-hearted towards each other.

The gentry will become grudgeful,
With respect to their trifling donations;
And blood relations will become cool towards each other,
Church livings shall become lay property.

All classes of people will be addicted to robbery,
Lords will become cold blooded murderers;
Ill-will and exclusive dealings,
Shall subsist between father and son.

Such is the description of the people,
Who shall live in the ages to come;
More unjust and iniquitous shall be
Every succeeding race of men!

The time shall come, &c.

SAINT COLUMBKILLE CECINIT

Hearken, thou, Boithin[1] with attention,
To the chime of my bell in chilling Hy!
Until I relate after having finished my psalmody,
Things that shall come to pass in the latter ages of the world.

Great carnage shall be made, justice shall be outraged,
Multitudinous evils, great suffering shall prevail, and many unjust
    laws will be administered,
Leath Cuind is causing great apprehension to me,
Above all other people upon the fair surface of the earth.

Though they shall be a pious noble race,
They shall be reduced to a state of distress in latter times,
A haughty clergy, and powerful kings,
Will cause their complete thraldom, and lasting sorrow.

Every act that shall cause their dispersion is decreed,
According to the will of the Son of the Blessed Virgin Mary,
* * * * *[2] a great event shall happen,
I fail not to notice it :—rectitude shall be its specious motive.

But if ye be not active pure,
A more sorrowful event cannot possibly happen;

---

[1] *Eisdse a Bhoithin.* This St. Boithin was a contemporary of St. Columbkille;
it was he that founded *Mainistear Boithin,* now Monasterboice, in the county
of Louth. A raving ignorant antiquary asserts that St. Boithin was no less a
personage than the river Boyne! and therefore imaginary; but there is a wide
difference between the names *Boithin* and *Boinn* (O'Kearney).

[2] illegible in manuscript.

Outside (despite), of Alba the mediatrix,
There shall be a defeat in the battle of the Lagenians.

There shall be a son of youth, a successful king[3],
He will be a noble personage, and an Archbishop,
On a Tuesday Cormac the gentle shall be slain,
Justice will be his object, and sincerity his pursuit.

Notwithstanding all circumstances it shall be on Thursday
The vital spark shall depart from the king's body :—
After that an illustrious person will come
From Meath, with a strong body of forces.

His power shall extend from shore to shore :
A fleet will arrive in Loch Ribh,
That fleet of Lock Ribh[4],
Shall prove advantageous to the stranger race.

The abbacy of Armagh shall be subject to them[5],
Their career shall be similar to that of sovereign princes,
Thirty years after that shall last,
The sovereignty of the Adulterer.

All will adhere to him to their disgrace,
Until he shall depart this life at Cloyne of Kiaran;
After that the Cairneach will assume the sovereignty,
Of Eire, without interruption.

---

[3] *Bu mac oige, &c.* This stanza relates to Cormac Mac Cuillenan Archbishop
of Cashel and King of Munster.

[4] *Is biait longus ar Loch Ribh, &c.* This stanza evidently alludes to the fleet
of the Norsemen that landed in Connacht.

[5] *Ba futha ab Ardmacha.* This stanza gives the desecration of Christian
Churches by the Danes who placed lay abbots in them, and the career of the
wicked Turgesius their king.

Fifteen years in vigour and purity,
Shall the CAIRNEACH[6] reign as supreme King;
Should the CAIRNEACH be counselled by me,
He, the liberal, the hilarious, the pious, and the hopeful,

He would avoid joining in the terrific struggle,
In which he will engage on Clontarf;
Clontarf, the field whereon shall be fought,
The very terrific, gory, tumultuous battle.

In consequence of which, multitudes of men shall be laid prostrate
    in gore,
Upon the field possessed by the wily man;
The Mael will afterwards appear,
He shall spring from a tribe in South Leinster.

Britain shall be tributary to him[7],—
A matter of fact that cannot be controverted,—
That same Mael of the unsheathed swords.
Will break the battle of Sliabh Grot.

That Mael, without struggle or prohibition,
Shall repel the king of Munster;
That king shall be the valiant CAIRNEACH,
Who will break the battle of Glen Madhma[8].

------

[6] *Cairneach* means a sacrificing priest, but is put here for a hero who made a great slaughter on his enemies; no doubt, Maelseachlain, king of Meath, is meant, since he succeeded the adulterer Turgesius. The subsequent stanzas show that Brian Boroimhe, who succeeded Maelseachlain, is also called a Cairneach.

[7] This stanza is not easily understood, unless we adopt the tradition often heard, that an Anglican king solicited aid from Brian, soon after he assumed the supreme government of Ireland, as genuine history.

[8] The battle of Glen Madhma was fought by Brian Boroimhe against the Danes and their allies.

He will immure the foreigners in their fortresses,
And will operate a change to their disadvantage;
Yet that same Mael, the son of DONN[9],
Shall prove injurious to Leith Cuinn, the seat of literature.

He will be hospitable and kind towards his friends,
But unfriendly towards strangers;
If this son of Donn would be advised by me,
He would not persecute Leith Cuinn[10].

Leith Cuinn renowned for warlike feats shall suffer,
Through the machinations of the treacherous murderer[11];
Though this sanguinary man will clearly discern
The consequences both near and afar.

This murderer, though a man of clear judgment,
Shall be slain by the hand of another murderer;
After that time the Fionn Bān will appear[12];
He will come from Munster—a great pest.—

---

[9] *Gi an Mael sin mac an Duinn.* Mael, in Irish, signifies a tonsured person, dedicated to the tutelage of a certain saint, or baptized under his or her special protection, as for instance, Mael-putruicc, servant or protégé of St. Patrick, Mael-Columb, the servant or protégé of St. Columbkille, Mael-Brighite, the servant of St. Bridget, &c. these cognomens became family names in after times, as Mul-patrick, or Fitzpatrick, Mael-Columb, or Malcolm, Mael-Bride, or Mac Mael Brighide, Mac Bride, &c. Donn signifies brown-haired. We are not aware whether Cineide, father of Brian, was or was not brown-haired; however, *donn* means also a valourous man; possibly this is the true meaning of the text.

[10] *Leith Cuinn,* Conn's half, the northern part of Ireland. *Leith Mogha,* the southern portion, or Mogha's half.

[11] *Fealltach fionngallach,* treacherous murderer. This epithet is not applied to Brian Boroimhe, but to his brother-in-law, Murchadh, king of Leinster, who richly deserved it.

[12] *Fionn ban,* Fionn the fair-haired. It is hard to guess who is meant by this Fionn, except Donogh son of Brian. He is said to come from Carricklea in Munster.

After hard struggles, and protracted warfare,
He will assume the sovereignty of two thirds of Ireland;
This furious Fionn from Carrick Leith,
Shall possess a spirit neither hesitative nor timid.

This person shall not meet a violent death—a great matter—
But shall die at Cinn-coradh;
After him, the son of Dall will assume[13]
The sovereignty of Meath—the son of Flann.—

Seven years in full power,
Shall the span of his sovereignty extend;
The son of Dall will be fortunate to meet friendship,
In the country of the strangers who afford only an unfriendly
    reception.

Though their arms shall be powerful in the north and south,
Maelgarbh will break down their confederacy;
Maelgarbh shall then obtain possession of Ireland,
Through the strength of his army.

During the life of his partner, he shall hold
Ireland without interruption in peace;
This same Maelgarbh, the handsome, shall be
The Maelgarbh who will disperse my pupils.

He will take the opportunity of a favourable time to disperse my
And will depredate my Derry[14];   pupils,

---

[13] This poem contains a prophecy, as may be seen, of the most remarkable kings who should hold principal sway in Ireland, but it is to be regretted we cannot enter on the history of the reign of those princes, in consequence of the cheapness of this edition, which we purpose for the use of the millions.

[14] *Mo Dhoire!* St. Columbkille, though in the island of Hy when he wrote this, could not forget his favourite Derry; and foreseeing the expulsion of its students and final despoilment, could not avoid exclaiming in the bitterness of his soul, "Oh my Derry! my beloved Derry," &c.

Oh, my Derry! my beloved little Derry!
My place of abode, and the solace of my existence!

Wo betide the man, O God, thou whose ways are unsearchable[15],
Who is destined to despoil my Derry!
There shall not be   *   *   *   *   *
*   *   *   *   *   *   *   *   *

After the despoilment of my beloved Derry,
And the dispersion of my pupils,
A Dalcassion[16] shall not obtain possession of Ireland,
Ever again—a long period of time.

The king who will cause a lasting change,
Shall be from Desmond—the prediction is correct—
Goodness for ever after that time;
And the sovereignty shall fall to the lot of Hugh Beanan.

This Maelgarbh, with a powerful body of forces,
Will depredate Tir-Eoghan renowned for arms;
Every tenth individual in Ireland
Shall die of plague during his reign!

This same Maelgarbh shall be seized on by the disease,
It shall be a terrific severe epidemic;
The prince shall die of that sickness
In the centre of Limerick of the fair plains.

---

[15] *Is mairg, &c.* The saint denounces heavenly vengeance upon the despoiler of his beloved Derry. Here the MS. was illegible and the omission is not supplied in any other that has as yet come to hand.

[16] *Ni gebfaid Dalccais, &c.* A Dalcascian shall never from the date of the destruction of the monastery of Derry, obtain the sovereignty of Ireland, because they have proved bad and degenerate monarchs, since the time of Brian. It should be observed before that *Maelgarbh* literally means *Rough Mael,* so called, probably, because those monarchs thus designated were bad and cruel men.

A man devoid of fear shall come from the north,
He will be vigorous, valiant and renowned for feats of arms;
He will obtain possession, though difficult to accomplish it,
Of Cruachan, Emain, and Oileach[17].

The DONN[18] will come from beyond Loch Leipheann[19],
It is he who shall obtain the sovereignty of Ireland;
Until he shall fall in a battle in Leinster,
On the eminence of Dun Saileach[20].

Multitudes of men in dense ranks will there attend,
On the day that my pupils shall be avenged;
From the time of the dispersion of my admirably intelligent pupils,
To that day shall number six score and fifteen years.

He who will there avenge the wrongs inflicted on my pupils,
Shall be he of the glossy ringletting locks from Fanat,
Hugh the magnanimous, the brown-haired, the irresistible,
The smooth-going chariot without blemish.

He of the ruddy countenance it is long until he is heard of—
The Defender, who will break down his enemy;

---

[17] *Cruacha, Emain, and Aileach.* Cruacha, written in English Cruachan, was the residence of the celebrated Maev Queen of Connacht; it was the residence of the kings of that province for many centuries. The word is often used to denote the whole province. Emain, situated near the present town of Armagh, was the royal residence of the Ultonian kings. Aileach was the royal residence of a branch of the family of O'Neill. Hugh O'Neill, the great Earl of Tyrone, is still believed to remain enchanted in the rock of Aileach, whence he with his troops, who are also supposed to be enchanted there, will rush upon the forces of the English, in their last struggle against the Irish people. A similar notion prevails respecting Gerald the fairy, Earl of Desmond.

[18] *Donn.* The name Donn is applied to a brave man, while that of Maelgarbh distinguishes a treacherous and cruel ruler.

[19] *Loch Leipheann* or *Leiphinn.* Loch Leane, situated about a mile from Fore, in the north-east of the county of Westmeath.

[20] *Dun Saileach,* properly Drum Saileach, an old name for Armagh.

The expert man of the race of Conn;
The successful hero, and the subduer of the Galls.

This will be Hugh the undaunted,
To whom the pillars of Tara shall submit;
He shall be remarkable for energy and wisdom,
He, the corner-stone (support) of every province in Ireland.

CATHAIR CONROI[21] (the city of Conroi) shall be ruined;—
It is a fact devoid of deception—
What a misfortune this to the hosts of Munster of the plains,
As well as to those of Limerick and Ceann-coradh[22]!

Seven and twenty years without error,
Shall the campaigns of Hugh[23] of the wonderous exploits continue;
According to arrangements made in the north and south,
He will break a battle every year.

One and twenty years with éclat,
Hugh shall reign as supreme king;
Hill and dale shall be subject to his sway,
And Ireland shall enjoy peace under his government.

The countenance of Hugh is familiar to me,
A face overshadowed with tressing locks of soft hair :
My intellect is confused, O Boithin,
If I thus sufficiently describe him.

_____

[21] *Cathair Conroi.* The city or residence of Conroi son of Daire (see his story in Keating). Its remains consist of a circle of large stones heaped up without mortar; it is situated on the summit of a mountain in the barony of Cork-aguiny, county of Kerry.

[22] *Ceann Coradh.* Kinkora, the residence of Brian Boroimhe, near Killaloe in the county of Clare.

[23] *Aedh.* Hugh. Probably Hugh O'Neill the great Earl of Ulster, who waged a successful war against Elizabeth, the virago of England.

Hugh will lead a body of troops from the north,
He, the king of Clann Connell of the well-tempered swords;
They will march to Dublin to force tribute,
From a young lady of the Galls[24] of bright shields.

Against them shall come from the east,
The king of the sea, the son of Godfrey;
He will pour a dreadful havoc upon them
From that place to the lake of Tir-da-bhan[25].

Throughout that battle, in which Hugh shall fall,
I assure you, though the information is sorrowful,
That when the Galls shall break forth,
Inevitable destruction shall stalk before them.

It is a cause of incessant pain to me—
And let all who hear it be convinced of its truth—
That Hugh the extraordinary shall fall,

*   *   *   *   *   *   *   *   *   *   *[26]

Thirty years after the reign of Hugh,
In the enjoyment of plenty and freedom,
Shall the country of hospitable houses remain—long till it is heard
    about—
Until Cliabh Glas[27] shall come into possession of it.

———

[24] This young lady of the Galls is unquestionably Queen Elizabeth, since we find by the text that Clann Conaill, or the great northern septs, were led against her by Aedh or Hugh.

[25] *Loch Tir-da-bhan*, probably Smerwick in Kerry is meant.

[26] The vellum MS was illegible here.

[27] *Cliabh Glas.* Grey chest; a name evidently given to the English invaders or their captain, probably on account of the colour of the suits of mail they wore,—*Glas*, green or grey—or because they came from the country of the Picts. Though it would seem to have reference to the Norsemen, whose sway over Ireland lasted about the period which is assigned to it, 189 years, still there are reasons for believing that the English invasion is meant, as in the

This Cliabh Glas will cause severe trials,
As he will be the cause of great disunion;
Be that as it will, the warrior will not be pusilanimous,
He who will kill the hoary man deprived of one eye.

Seven kings, after Cliabh Glas the upright,
Shall hold possession of the Island of Heremon;
Seven and twenty years, without error,
Shall pass between the sovereignity of each supreme king.

The last of those kings, who shall hold sway,
Over proud Ireland of the elevated mountains,
The country renowned for poetry and prosperity,
Flann Ciotach[28] (blood-showering) will come upon them.

For a long time every king will be a Flann Ciotach,
Who shall assume the sovereignty of Eirin;
It is in his time the garment of death will descend,
And the rowing wheels[29] will arrive.

Ten hundred compartments shall be in the fleet;
It shall contain a number of true friends who cannot be repelled;
The number of sincere friends shall be extraordinary,
Each compartment shall contain ten hundred men !

---

language of prophecy time is seldom intelligibly defined, and though it mentions Clontarf in plain terms, the *Rotha Ramha,* rowing wheels, manifestly alluding to *steam paddles,* did not arrive in the time of the conflict with the Danes on Clontarf. In all probability the text has allusion to a second battle on Clontarf, on which occasion the city of Magh Nealty, Dublin, shall be burned.

[28] *Flann Ciotach,* a name by which a savage, blood-stained tyrant is designated.

"For a long time every king will be a Flann Ciothach,
  Who shall assume the sovereignty of Ireland."

[29] Rowing wheel, evidently the paddle of a steam vessel—since the peculiar description of the fleet is given in the following stanza. This is ample proof that the past battle on Clontarf is not the one alluded to. *Vide supra, note* 27, p. 122.

The armament will spread its forces over sea and land,
The men composing this strange hostile fleet;
Nor will it (the fleet) divest its bosoms of garments,
Until it will rear up mounds with mangled bones!

They will inflict on their enemies without deception,
To such a degree that scarce a man of them shall escape
A severe flesh-hewing course of warfare,
Across the wide-extending sea.

The Galls will muster on Magh Ealta[30],
Exulting in the valour of their arms;
A keen-edged sword, their weak policy,
The Gael will cleave the head of the Gall.

The fleet of rowing wheels will remain after that,
Two short years and a half;
It is evident that a more respectable race never existed,
Than that of the fleet of Inbhir Domhnain[31].

This fleet that will come across the sea shall consist
Of ten ships, ten hundred fairy barks[32];
Ten hundred boats; ten hundred cock-boats;
And ten hundred capacious skiffs!

It (the fleet) will twice circumnavigate Eirin,
A truth devoid of any deception;
The principal seaport belonging to the country abroad,
Shall look to the west of Inbhir Domhnain.

---

[30] *Magh-Ealta.* The ancient name of Clontarf.

[31] *Inbhir Domhnain,* or bay of Sligo. This fleet shall remain in this country during two and a-half years.

[32] Fairy barks, another name given to this strange fleet of steam vessels.

They will gather together, a bold piece of policy,
The herds and women of the Gaedhal;
Prosperous shall be the career of their forces,
Until they arrive near Tara.

Flann Ciothach will there overtake them,
And the degenerate will not be timid :
He will pour out upon them battle and a hard contested struggle,
At a place contiguous to the Rath of Cormac[33].

They will all engage in a battle on the plain,
The Galls and the Gaels,
Close to the ford in the valley,
The battle shall fall but little short of a mutual carnage.

O Boithin the amiable devoid of harshness,
They will all burn with a flame of mutual affection;
It is a consolation to my heart without any disappointment.
That the Galls shall be worsted in the battle.

They will pursue them with their ships,
Over the mountain-billowy ocean;
So that no more shall escape them with life,
Except the crew of one bark, O Boithin !

The issue shall be that during the seven score years[34],
The sovereignty of this people shall continue;
They shall be exceedingly prosperous during that period,
Until the fires on St. John's eve be lighted.

------

[33] *Rath Cormac*. An old name of the hill of Tara, where the English forces shall fight a sanguinary battle, with the invaders and Irish, as described in the text.

[34] *Dil na seacht b-fithchitt ud.* During these seven score years, prophetic dates cannot be other than mystical. See, for instance, the days of the Old Testament as a prophetical chronology.

The festival of Saint John[35] shall fall on a Friday,
When the young men of many races shall be expelled;
They will settle eastward in the Tyrian sea,
They shall obtain only a fourth part.

I concede as a favour to them without deception,
And St. Patrick also did concede the same;
That seven years before the last day,
The sea shall submerge Eirin by one inundation.[36]

---

[35] Until the fires on St. John's eve be burned It must be confessed that this expression much favours the general traditional history relative to the discomfiture of the Danish power in Ireland. It is recorded that when the Irish, after the death of Turgesius, resolved on a general massacre of their enslavers, that they, by a preconcerted signal, agreed to light fires upon every rath and hill throughout Ireland, which incident was a warning that all the people were to massacre the *bonachts,* or Danish soldiers cantoned upon them. This was done, and, in commemoration of the event, the fires of Bealtine, or the eve of May-day, had been ever since that period held on the eve of St. John's day. the eve on which the event took place, except in Dublin and its vicinity, which was then the stronghold of the Danes. Hence the May fires are still held on that eve and not on that of St. John. This tradition is, indeed, a very plausible one; but beyond tradition we find no written account of any such massacre of the Norsemen having taken place; and more, there are reasons for thinking that the fires lighted on the eve of St. John the Baptist's day had been lighted in honour of the sun long before the light of Christianity dawned upon this country. At all events, if the text has any reference to the expulsion of the Danes from Ireland, it is certain that the stanzas have been disarranged; and. if they have, such disarrangement must have taken place many centuries ago. In any event it is more than probable that present belligerent parties will adopt different interests to those advocated by them at present.

[36] This stanza alludes to one of the petitions granted by the Almighty to St. Patrick, after having expelled the demons from Ireland, namely, that the surrounding ocean should submerge Ireland seven years before the day of doom, so that Antichrist could possess no power over the people. This was considered a great blessing, and is mentioned in the Leabhar Breac, fol. 14 b. thus:— "*Acus co ti muir tarsa uii. m-bliadna ria m-brat.*" *A*nd the sea shall overwhelr it (Ireland) seven years before the judgment. The same is recorded as the fin: doom of Ireland in the *Irish Nennius,* edited by Rev. Dr. Todd for the Iri Archæological Society, p. 218, in nearly the same words:—"*Muir tairsi u*

The angels in Heaven will celebrate
The vespers of my festival on a Thursday;—
I with sincerity offer to the King of the heavenly luminaries,
These predictions which I leave to posterity.

Though another may feel a commotion similar to mine,
I shall suffer the penalty of the dread :
Thus shall be without doubt or folly,
The world and the king of heaven.

I am Columb, a descendant of the illustrious Niall,
O Boithin of the pure life;
(Those things) were clearly manifested to myself,
A week from this day (on which) you hear them..

HEARKEN THOU.

---

m-bliadna re m-brath," translated thus:—"The sea will come over it seven years before the day of judgment," p. 219. John O'Connell, in his *Poem on Ireland*, alludes to that event in the following terms:—

Lest the deceptions, snares and danger
Of Antichrist should fall upon the Irish;
He (the Almighty) promised to send a deluge over Ireland,
Seven years previous to the burning of the spheres (globes).

Ralph Higden (Polychron. lb. 5, cap. 4) has recorded the tradition, that St Patrick obtained for the Irish the singular privilege, that no Irishman shall be alive during the reign of Antichrist. This serves to explain the expectation that the sea shall cover Ireland seven years before the day of judgment.

THE THREE CONNS[1]

St. Columbkille cecinit

The three Conns, the descendants of Ruadh[2]
Of the race of Conall of great power;
It is from the paternal stock of that man,
The magnates of that stock shall derive their worth.

The first Conn of these shall be, as I opine,
A king whose race shall be troublesome and short;
His career shall be productive of little advantage to himself,
Though he will be prosperous while heir presumptive to the crown.

---

[1] The Three Conns. The great men who should hold the supreme power in Ireland are predicted in this prophetical poem. It is indeed difficult to give any correct comment upon it, but it is evident that Brian Boroimhe was one of the three Conns, and Hugh O'Neill, earl of Tyrone, another. Many a leader of the olden time fancied that he was one of the Conns, whose career had been predicted by the saint; and a celebrated warrior of the invading Saxons used to carry the poem with him, believing himself to be the third. It is evident, however, that two of those great men have passed away, and their achievements are now matters of history; yet some few learned in native lore think that one great warrior shall come forward in time to come, but it is to be feared that they are mistaken.

[2] *Ruadh*, a red-haired person; the word also means famous, renowned. *Clan Conall,* race or descendants of Conall, the O'Donnells, and other families of distinction in Tir-connell, so called after Conall Gulban. The idea of a great liberator of Ireland arising from the family of the O'Donnells in the person of *Ball-Dearg O Domhnaill* (Red-Spot O'Donnell), because tradition states that a branch of that family had an hereditary red spot on their persons, so popular in the north, may have originated with this poem. It is indeed the most hard used up (*sic*), and variously interpreted of any of the prophetic poems of our saint.

In a derout, though a matter of great consequence,
He himself and his troops shall fall,
At a small isthmus between two arms of the sea,
About noontide, by the clann of Eoghan[3].

The second Conn, though he shall be tardy,
Shall be a prince in every respect;
By his stolid crazed paternal people,
He, together with his power, shall fall.

The third Conn, a man of unimpeded career,
The honest, liberal Fionn (fair-haired,) from Fanat[4]
Will promote the extent of his dominions by sea and land,
Up to Carn-Ui-Neid in Munster.

During three years with successful sway,
Shall he reign monarch of Ireland from south to north;
A bright crozier will not be unveiled against him,
Nor a peal of bells unmuffled.

He will form an alliance with another people,
From the northwards of Cantire;
They will make a descent upon the Isle of Man, of the banquets,
To wreak vengeance upon that people for their ancestors.

He will break down their bulwarks,
And raze to the ground their fortified places;
The news of which shall be carried across the sea,
To the king of the Saxons in London.

---

[3] *Cineal Eoghain.* The Momonians; so called from Eoghan Mor, who forced
Conn of the Hundred Battles to divide the kingdom with him by a line or
boundary made from Dublin to Galway; the northern half being Conn's and the
southern Eoghan's.

[4] Fanet, a district of considerable extent in the north, once the patrimony of
the Mac Sweenys.

That king will despatch a great body of forces,
Against them, without any deception;
He will force his tributes, with relentless might,
From the noble Galls of Ireland.

That expedition from the east will rendezvous,
On the old Magh Ealta of Binn-Eadair;
The Galls of Meath and of the great towns,
Will come and join their muster.

An alliance will be there entered into,
Between the Galls of this country and the Danair (Easterlings),
They will then proclaim war without any pretext,
Against the men of Ireland and Alba, (Scotland).

That proclamation of war shall be unwise;
For in consequence of it battle shall be broken upon themselves,
And they shall not afterwards regain prosperity,
Until the time of their final reduction.

Such a large assemblage of men,
Never before met either in the east or west;
And never again shall such a muster congregate,
While Ireland is a seagirt Island.

Though one may there meet his next akin,
He will, alas! forget the ties of kindred,
And they too shall be there affected with the same forgetfulness,
The pure Danair and the Geraldines!

Neither will Conn be mindful of his kindred race,
* * * * by means of them, without error;
The carnage shall be almost general,
On Magh Ealta (Clontarf,) of the garments.

They will be slain by the clanns of Conn,
And by the people descended from Oilioll Olum;

The descendants of Labhra Lorc will aid in their destruction,
On Magh Ealta contiguous to their encampment.

The city of Magh Ealta will be set on fire,
A most lamentable spectacle to behold!
The Galls renowned for their fleets shall be broken down,
And my Liberator Conn shall fall!

I cannot observe after the death of Conn,
Aught but a sameness among his kindred clans—
Until the son of Ruadh (red-haired), from the glen appear,
The span of the kingly reign shall be but brief.

After the blameless son of Ruadh,
Cathbarr from Cruachin shall assume the sovereign power,
Though many fraudulent acts will be committed during his reign,
He will be upon the whole a friend to the church.

The celebrated race of Heber will arrive there,
And the clann of IR of the gold-decked accoutrements,
Grecians[5] will afterwards arrive,
Anl the people descended from Ith, the son of Breogan.

It is thus the tide of affairs shall principally flow,
O'Boithin of the most amiable countenance,—
They were the angels of the living God,
Who made manifest to me the history of the three Conns.

THE THREE CONNS.

---

[5] *Greiga,* Greeks; who those Grecians may be. it is difficult to conjecture, it may be one of the many results which spring from war. By the people descended from Ith, son of Breogan the Spaniards and Portuguese were evidently meant.

THE FALL OF TARA[1]

COLUMBKILLE CECINIT

Tara of Magh Bregia which you now see so prosperous,
Shall be covered with grass—all its buildings as well as its elevated
   site,
It shall not be long ere it becomes a desert,
Though it is today in the enjoyment of prosperous affluence!

I assure you in serious verity,
O Tara, the flourishing seat of monarchy,
That there is not to-night on the wide expanse of Banba
A place, alas! fated to enjoy such brief stability.

The repulsive denials there met from day to day,
Strongly excite my charitable complement;
Prosperity will forsake its hills,
In consequence of the rudeness and inhospitality that there prevails.

---

[1] Fall of Tara. This poem was composed by our saint on the occasion of his pleading before Aedh, monarch of Ireland, to free Aidan, king of the Albanian Scots, from the tribute long imposed upon his people, when the Irish monarch refused to remit that galling tribute imposed upon the Irish who colonised a portion of Alba or Scotland. On the stern refusal of the monarch Aedh to grant an indemnity of the tribute, the saint arose, and before the king and chiefs assembled, foretold the downfall of Tara, then the most magnificent seat of royalty in Europe, confuted the haughty monarch to his face by showing the vanity of the pomp of the world, especially in the downfall of Tara, and the total instability of human affairs. His address had the desired effect. Some centuries after this Tara was cursed by St. Ruadan, and was therefore abandoned, so that, according to the prophecy of our saint, Tara was no more the seat of a king or chief.

To a place where neither people nor dwellings are found
None will resort to solicit a favour;
Sorrow must await those who make bad use of their means,
And share not with the necessitous.

Wo betide those who practise repulsiveness and refusals
Who repel the peasant and the prince alike;
It is the penalty which the acts of princes earned,
That Tara shall be devoid of a house for ever.

Oileach and Tara, now seats of power,
Rath-cruachin, and Eamhain[2] the lofty;
Shall be deserted, though now so replenished,
To such an extent that a roof-tree shall not remain on the raths.

The chief cause of this downfall shall be—
As the King of kings hath assured to me—
Because the chiefs of Ireland of the slender towers,
Do not believe in CHRIST without hesitation.

It shall not so happen to the saints,
Who are in compact with Him of the benign countenance
The joys prepared for them will increase each day,
In Heaven without any deception.

I assure you, without fear of contradiction—
For I have the information from my Heavenly King—
That no one shall find either a king or prince,
Or obtain food or drink within the walls of Tara.

TARA OF MAGH BREGIA.

---

[2] *Oileach, Rath-Cruachin, Eamhain,* seats of royalty.

EIRE THIS NIGHT

COLUMBKILLE CECINIT

How prosperous Eire is this night !
Her immense substance is free from taxation,
Her princes are hospitable, her palaces are full,
Her people numerous, and her crops productive[1].

Though this Eire is so prosperous this night,
A time will come when she will be reduced to destitution;
A powerful force of strangers will invade her,
From Lochlan of the sea-faring Galls[2].

They will entertain kind feelings towards no person,
Their hordes will take possession of every house;
Prolific shall be the race that will come across the seas,
The Danair (Danes), will be resolute fierce warriors[3].

Long shall their sway continue over the island of Conn;
They shall be the less benignant of any race of people;
They will prevail both by sea and land,
And will destroy the navy of our enterprising kings[4].

---

[1] This stanza gives a true description of the prosperous state of Ireland, while governed by her own kings, and in the enjoyment of her proper liberties.

[2] The Danes and Norwegians. *Gall,* a name for all foreigners; *Gael,* for Irishman.

[3] A true picture of the barbarous pagan Norsemen is given in this stanza.

[4] *Loingeas,* &c. It little signifies what has been said and written to the contrary, our monarchs maintained a splendid fleet. The Irish fleet was found in Gaul, Britain, Lochlan, &c. conveying troops, and the Irish were the first discoverers of Iceland, where they resorted to fish for cod, and it was by the

The time shall come, it is no tribulation to me,
When their doom shall be sealed, and their further career impeded;
(For,) on Clontarf[5] of the blood stained garments,
Battle shall be broken upon them in one day.

Another race of invaders will come hither across the seas[6],
Their number shall be few, though their power prove great,
Six hundred years and ninety more in full,
Shall they impose their tributes upon us.

They will take possession of a portion of Ireland,
Their progress shall be but slow in the beginning;
But they will forcibly extend their supremacy,
With a lubriciousness similar to that of a mist stealing upon a
    headland.

They will persecute the Gaels with galling ferocity;
Their petitions for restitution will be disregarded,
This grievance shall stir up the descendants of Conn,
With the descendants of Eoghan of the diadems of gold.

The native Irish shall be reduced to the condition of sojourners
    during their sway,
They shall be deprived of their rights, instead of enjoying their
    dignities,
Whole tribes will be annihilated; their laws shall be unjust,
Plotting shall constitute the main features of their career.

———

Irish America was first discovered and, most probably, partly peopled, *vid.*
Crymogea, Johnston, Norse Antiq., and MS. edition of the Battle of Clontarf,
in the library of the Royal Irish Academy.

[5] The Norsemen were worsted and their power broken down by Brian
Boroimhe in the Battle of Clontarf, fought on Good-Friday, A.D. 1014, *vid.*
MS. Battle of Clontarf, and Irish history, &c.

[6] This alludes to the English invasion. The number of invaders who first
landed in Ireland were few indeed, but they imperceptibly spread themselves
over the country, like a mist stealing in from the sea upon a mountain.

They will erect lime-built towers[7] upon every headland,
Their kings will be treacherous, their nobles powerful;
They will noose halters around the necks of every person;
Such shall be the results of the injustice and litigiousness of the
                                                          stranger.

An uninterrupted course of warfare will mark their career,
While their keen-edged swords shall be ever reeking with blood;
Fire, robbery, and every species of infliction will prevail,
They will persecute the Gael into exile.

Hard fought bloody wars will be waged,
But the Gael shall be the most frequently discomfitted;
To their degenerate spirit and internal dissensions,
Their downfall and subsequent sufferings may be attributed.

An uncultivated language will be found in every person's mouth[8]
Proud abbots (clergy) will rule over every sanctified church:
In both north and south iron wheels shall support[9],
Fiery chariots, which shall resemble druidical deception.

In the last ninety years of (Irish) bondage[10],
A man from Munster will start into notoriety;
Though he shall be neither a prince, a soldier, nor a lord,
Every person will send him tribute to Dublin.

---

[7] This has allusion to the castles and other fortifications built by the English
settlers for the purposes of securing their conquests, or robberies, and of awing
the natives into some sort of submission.

[8] The English tongue has been condemned by all Irish writers, and considered
a mere jargon, which it really is when compared to their own copious, sweet,
polished language. Proud abbots—the protestant clergy who took forcible possession of the abbeys and churches are here meant.

[9] Our railway carriages, "fiery chariots that would resemble the deception
caused by the operation of magic." It was always traditionally recorded that
chariots without the aid of horses would traverse the country.

[10] This and the following two stanzas plainly describe the life, career, and
death of Ireland's liberator, Daniel O'Connell; also the state of parties after
his demise—extraordinary—I did not well understand this when I made this
translation more than eight years ago in 1856.

136

During his career power will be measured with power,
He will relieve the families belonging to high septs;
He will afterwards cross the boundless sea,
And he shall fall in a foreign country!

After his decease deception will prevail over the land of Fail,
To such an extent that no friendly associations will exist;
No man can calculate upon the support of a friend,
Any more than he can rely upon that of his sworn enemy.

A pure Cleric without reproach will appear[11],
Who will prohibit the use of darkening (intoxicating) drinks,
Like the full moon amidst the lesser luminaries,
Shall the dignity of this foster-father appear.

Storms, plagues, and gnawing famine shall prevail,
The seasons will not observe their regular course;
Plague will consume the powerful as well as the weak,
With painful cramps of one half day's duration[12]!

Dearth will become oppressive throughout the land,
Though there shall be abundance of food on one part (side)[13];
Thousands shall die of starvation—houses shall be full,
Afterwards the land shall become a barren waste.

Persons of substance shall be reduced to a state of insolvency,
No bankers will supply them with the necessary funds;
A fraudulent system of trade will enhance their ruin,
And they shall afterwards be left to weep in sorrow.

---

[11] This is Father Theobald Mathew, without any doubt.

[12] The cholera morbus.

[13] *The houses shall be filled.* This means either that stores shall be filled with provisions, though the people shall perish of famine by thousands, or that poor-houses shall be filled with agricultural labourers and their families.

The pure fair Gael will fly away[14]
Into exile into both the eastern and western regions of the world;
The scantiness of land, and oppressive debts, without a falsehood,
Shall bring decay upon them, day by day.

The dignities assumed by nobles and great men shall be subverted,
The nobility shall sink into humble life before the great war[15];
That war that will be proclaimed against them from beyond the seas,
By means of which the franticly-proud race shall be subdued.

Legislators will enact fatal and unjust statutes,
To deprive the rightful clergy of church dignities;
(For) they will look upon their fame as an impediment in their way,
Misfortunes and mortifications shall afterwards become their portion.

The laws will be enacted in a spirit of gross injustice;
The clergy of the holy church will be persecuted
By the false-hearted Galls both here and abroad,
Which event will cause great excitement in every place.

The leading men and clergy shall be aroused in consequence of
those enactments,
They will make a noisy remonstrance;
Nothing they will do shall avail themselves,
Except to the detriment of the enemy.

The enemies of the Galls shall be aroused into activity[16],
They who reside in the eastern and western parts of the world;

---

[14] The wholesale emigration of the oppressed Irish. No further comment is needed.

[15] All our saints foretold that this great war which should ruin England shall be proclaimed by some powerful foreign potentate; some people say that it shall be a religious war. Time shall tell more than we can at present.

[16] The injustice of England in all her relations, more especially those respecting Ireland, shall arouse foreign nations both in the eastern and western parts

So that they will engage in a battle on the circumscribed sea,
In consequence of which they (Galls) shall be scattered (defeated).

A fleet belonging to a foreign country will come hither,
Manned by the descendants of Golimh[17] of the gold-embroidered
    garments,
They shall lay prostrate the Galls of the ships,
And liberate the people who have been held in bondage.

---

of the globe to put a final end to her intermeddling domineering career. Here is a fragment of a song written on our prophecies by the celebrated Irish bard, Peter O'Dorin, on the occasion of Arthur Brownlow, Esq. of Lurgan, ancestor of the present Lord Lurgan, having contested the representation of the county of Armagh with the Achesons of Markethill, and other powerful opponents. The bard states the final downfall of England, and more particularly the puerility of supporting any one candidate in preference to another It has been stated by persons deserving credit that the Rev. William Neilson, D.D. and a catholic clergyman offered forty guineas for a perfect copy of this ballad; but it could not be had. The following fragment is all we have been able to collect, and it may be worth preserving.

THE INDEPENDENT MAN

"When powers agree, 'tis then you shall see,
   That with sudden career on Britain they'll come;
They'll pell-mell all three, not sparing degree,
   The grey and the green with bullet and drum.
While on their career, I'll laugh and I'll sneer,
   Enjoying good cheer, I'll sip of my rum;
Yet devoid of all fear, I'll sit like a peer,
   With my bottle of beer *un*-undher my thumb."

ON ELECTIONEERING, he says:—

"In Heaven's great name! how can they blame,
   The poor man, or shame him, in the long run?
Ambition's their game, what else do they mean,
   But purchase high fame, great power, and fun?
They may swear a big oath, that never they'll loath,
   The poor dupe that votes for them : 'tis their plan,
But I'll keep my own vote; I'll give it to none,
   Then what need I care for a parliament-man?"

[17] Golimh was the great ancestor of the Milesian race; the Spaniards, Portuguese, &c. were considered as the kinsmen of the old Irish.

This fleet that will arrive here from the east,
Cannot be impeded on the mighty ocean;
Through the impetuosity of its noisy breathing[18],
Its strange appearance shall be marked by flaming mouths.

They will engage in a furious conflict,
Who compose the fleet of Balina[19];
It shall be a wonder that it will not be a mutual slaughter,
The conflict of those who will come hither to sever the intricate knot.

The Galls will muster their ruthless forces with resolution
After their bloody hard-contested sea-fight;
On Magh-dair[20] of the druid,
It is then the battle of Mullagh-mast[21] will be fought.

---

[18] Through the impetuosity of its noisy breathing. Probably the rumbling noise of escaping steam.—*flaming mouths*, the chimneys or engineering departments of steam ships.

[19] Balina may be the name of any port where a river empties itself into the sea; but it also is the name of Ballina in the Co. Mayo. There can be no reason for associating this expedition with that of the French fleet in 1798, inasmuch as that fleet was not composed of steam vessels. In another place St Columbkille says, "this battle shall be fought in the morning by the men of Connacht." That battle is not yet fought. *After the hard contested sea fight;* all the authorities we have been able to consult agree that the English shall sustain a great defeat by sea, not in the English Channel or Irish Sea, but in some narrow eastern sea, perhaps in the Mediterranean. The English fleet has suffered considerably in the eastern waters already. It is clear that, though the flame of the English maritime power was great, and deserved unbounded praise for its efficiency, its day has past over, and its old hulks cannot now compete with the ships of America or even of France, as they are newly built on the most approved systems invented in ship-building.

[20] It appears from the text that Kildare had been called *Dara*, or *Daru*, from a druid of that name, and not from *dair*, an oak, as is generally supposed. There has been a very prevalent tradition that the Curragh of Kildare shall be the scene of bloodshed, in consequence of the Irish army refusing to go abroad. Whether the prediction about the present encampment there, which we heard foretold a thousand times over, has been founded on this text, we cannot tell, but if we give credit to many other texts, we can see that the English, as a last resource, shall muster their forces some place near the Curragh, and will come to the determination to conquer or die. This determination

140

After the Galls shall be defeated in this battle[22],
They shall be harassed from every quarter;
Like a fawn surrounded by a pack of voracious hounds,
Shall be the position of the Saxons amidst their enemies.

---

is laconically expressed in tradition thus: "It shall be much easier to hew an oak with a pen-knife, than displace the son of a Gall from his saddle," so resolute will they be. But when the enemy shall appear, the tradition adds:— "They shall become as weak as a woman in travail before their enemy." It may as well be said here that this tradition respecting the resolute bearing of the English troops and their subsequent dismay is much localised; for instance, it is said that their courage shall be wound up to the highest pitch in the streets of Ardee; but that courage shall die away when they proceed some short distance, and discern the great strength of the enemy, augmented by the enchanted troops of *Gearoitt Jarla,* (Garrett or Gerald), who is said to have been enchanted in a small hill near Ardee, called *Mullagh Elim.* This Earl is now generally supposed to have been of the Kildare branch; this is an error; he was Garrett great Earl of Desmond, commonly called the fairy earl, because he was supposed to have been skilled in magic; he governed the earldom of Desmond 30 years, and died A.D. 1339, vide Dom. Rosari, O'Daly's work, translated by Rev. C. P. Meehan, p. 35. In a fairy poem in my possession, the raid of Gerald Jarla and his troops is thus recorded:—

> When the bloody mills operate,
> Without a drop of aught but blood,
> Earl Gerald, mounted on his bald black steed will arise,
> And take revenge for the blood that was spilled,
> On the eve of Sunday at Aughrim—
> It is then the war will come to Ireland.

This, however, deserves but little credit, as it is a piece of pythonic faticination, and not genuine prophecy, though there are hundreds, in the memory of persons still living, who used to assert that they had many audiences with the fairy earl.

[21] An ancient moat constructed on a hill about five miles east of Athy, county of Kildare. It is now called Mullaghmast, noted for a treacherous massacre of Irish chiefs by the hands of the English in the reign of Elizabeth. It appears that another great battle will be fought near this place; perhaps the battle of the plains of Kildare is meant; allusion is elsewhere made to this battle.

[22] This stanza contains a fearful description of the state to which the English will be reduced; they will, no doubt, be paid home a long reckoning by their oppressed colonies, &c. in the time of their weakness. The great rain immediately following this stanza laconically depicts the condition of an arch-tyrant in the last stage of his existence.

The Saxons afterwards shall dwindle down into a disreputable people,
And every obstacle shall be opposed to their future prosperity:
Because they did not observe justice and rectitude,
They shall be for ever after deprived of power!

Three warnings will be given them before their final fall,
The burning of the Tower of the great kings,
The conflagration of the Dockyard of the Galls,
And the burning of the Treasury where gold is deposited[23].

This new Eire shall be Eire the prosperous,
Great shall be her renown and her power;
There shall not be on the surface of the wide earth,
A country found to equal this fine country!

EIRE THIS NIGHT, &c.

---

[23] *Three warnings* will be conceded to the English to prepare them for their final downfall, namely the burning of the Tower of Kings, or Tower of London, the burning of the Dock-yard, and the destruction of the Treasury, or Bank; the two former have already been given, but the third is yet to come.